Trends in Functional Programming

Volume 5

Edited by
Hans-Wolfgang Loidl
Ludwig-Maximilians University, Munich

intellect
Bristol, UK
Portland, OR, USA

First published in the UK in 2006 by
Intellect Books, PO Box 862, Bristol BS99 1DE, UK.
First published in the USA in 2006 by
Intellect Books, ISBS, 920 NE 58th Ave. Suite 300, Portland, Oregon 97213-3786,
USA.

A catalogue record for this book is available from the British Library

ISBN 1-84150-144-1
ISSN 1743-4505 (Print)

Printed and bound in Great Britain by 4edge Ltd.

Contents

Preface

The fifth installment of the 'Trends in Functional Programming' series was the first one to be organised outside Scotland, the homeland of functional programming that hosted previous installments of TFP and the precursor series, the 'Scottish Functional Programming Workshops', going back to 1989. In November 2004, Ludwig-Maximilians University, Munich was the host for TFP04. With the change of venue we had a broad spectrum of submissions both in terms of contents and nationality of the authors: in total 22 papers have been submitted for presentation, and TFP04 itself was attended by 36 participants from 13 countries.

The Symposium on Trends in Functional Programming (TFP) is dedicated to promoting new research directions related to the field of functional programming and to investigate the relationships of functional programming with other branches of computer science. It is designed to be a platform for novel and upcoming research, combined with a post-event refereeing process and a formal publication of selected papers as a book. The presentations submitted this year show a wide spectrum of current research within this scope, from theoretical work on foundations of programming languages to practical usage of functional languages in many different domains.

Reflecting our dedication to promote the work by young researchers in this field, the programme committee for TFP has selected this year for the first time a student paper for the 'Best Student Paper' award. We are glad to announce that for TFP04 this award goes to:

Ron van Kesteren, Marko van Eekelen, Maarten de Mol
'Proof Support for General Type Classes'

We hope that this award will be even more motivation for all young researchers to produce high-quality papers describing their work and to present it in an international forum.

The papers in this volume of TFP cover a wide range of topics from theory, formal aspects of functional programming, graphics and visual programming to distributed computing and compiler design. As is often the case in this community, the most prolific work comes out of the combination of theoretical work with its application on classical problems in functional programming.

The distinguished paper by van Kesteren et al. in Chapter 1 is a good example of this combination, developing proof methods in the SPARKLE system in order to prove properties common to all instances of a Haskell type class. One fruitful and very active area of functional languages at the moment is generic programming. In Chapter 2, Reig presents a methodology for proving common properties of such generic programs, phrased in type classes within Haskell. The work of Dubois et al. on the FOCAL system in Chapter 3 follows a similar overall direction, integrating proving support into a high-level functional language and supporting advanced language features in the proving component of the integrated system.

Any formal treatment of modern programming languages has to cope with the presence of many different language concepts, and thus concrete formalisations often become unwieldy. In Chapter 4, Hutton and Wright demonstrate how to introduce exceptions into a simple abstract machine by performing equational reasoning on its high-level specification. In Chapter 5, Ghani et al. discuss the category theoretic foundations of combinators such as fold and augment, and extend their results to a wider class of inductive types using these combinators.

The core areas for the TFP series of programming language design and implementation are covered by several papers. In Chapter 6, Rossberg et al. present a functional language for distributed computation, using classical concepts such as futures for synchronisation. In Chapter 7, Németh presents a detailed empirical analysis of the performance of the GHC Haskell compiler, with varying orderings of the optimisation phases, and identifies orderings that consistently improve performance over the default setting for maximal optimisation. In Chapter 8, Evers et al. present a method for the better separation of the logic and the layout of GUI-level forms, and present a library providing an added level of abstraction. Finally, Clerici and Zoltan present in Chapter 9 NiMo, a graphic programming language based on dataflow graphs using lazy evaluation, which provides support for debugging and step-wise program development in its visual programming environment.

Hans-Wolfgang Loidl,
Munich

Acknowledgements

I would like to thank Martin Hofmann and the other members of the Theoretical Computer Science group of the Department for Informatics at the Ludwig-Maximilians University, Munich, for the help in promoting and organising TFP04. I am indebted to Max Jakob and Spyridon Iliopoulos for valiant on-site help during TFP04. I am particularly grateful to the members of the programme committee and all the referees for a smooth refereeing process. The programme committee for TFP04 was comprised of:

- Stephen Gilmore, University of Edinburgh
- Gaetan Hains, Universite d'Orleans
- Kevin Hammond, University of St Andrews
- John Hughes, Chalmers University
- Hans-Wolfgang Loidl, Ludwig-Maximilians-University Munich (Chair)
- Rita Loogen, Philipps-University Marburg
- Greg Michaelson, Heriot-Watt University Edinburgh
- John O'Donnell, University of Glasgow
- Ricardo Pena, Universidad Complutense de Madrid
- Phil Trinder, Heriot-Watt University Edinburgh
- Marko van Eekelen, University of Nijmegen
- Phil Wadler, University of Edinburgh

Further thanks go to the members of the TFP steering committee for general advice and concrete help in running this event. Last, but not least, I want to thank all participants of TFP04 for making this year's symposium such a lively event and for making it worth the while for me to organise it.

I am happy to acknowledge financial support by the EU through the APPSEM II Thematic Network and the Mobile Resource Guarantees project, funded as IST-2001-33149 under the European Commission's Fifth Framework Programme.

Chapter 1

Proof Support for General Type Classes

Ron van Kesteren[1], Marko van Eekelen[1], Maarten de Mol[1]

Abstract: We present a proof rule and an effective tactic for proving properties about HASKELL type classes by proving them for the available instance definitions. This is not straightforward, because instance definitions may depend on each other. The proof assistant ISABELLE handles this problem for single parameter type classes by structural induction on types. However, this does not suffice for an effective tactic for more complex forms of overloading. We solve this using an induction scheme derived from the instance definitions. The tactic based on this rule is implemented in the proof assistant SPARKLE.

1.1 INTRODUCTION

It is often stated that formulating properties about programs increases robustness and safety, especially when formal reasoning is used to prove these properties. Robustness and safety are becoming increasingly important considering the current dependence of society on technology. Research on formal reasoning has spawned many general purpose proof assistants, such as COQ [dt04], ISABELLE [NPW02], and PVS [OSRSC99]. Unfortunately, these general purpose tools are geared towards mathematicians and are hard to use when applied to more practical domains such as actual programming languages.

Because of this, proof assistants have been developed that are geared towards specific programming languages. This allows proofs to be conducted on the source program using specifically designed proof rules. Functional languages are especially suited for formal reasoning because they are referentially transpar-

---

[1]Nijmegen Institute for Computing and Information Sciences, Radboud University Nijmegen, Toernooiveld 1, Nijmegen, 6525 ED, The Netherlands; Phone: +031 (0)24-3653410; E-mail: rkestere@sci.ru.nl, M.vanEekelen@niii.ru.nl, M.deMol@niii.ru.nl

```
class Eq a where
  (==) :: a -> a -> Bool

instance Eq Int where
  x == y = predefinedeqint x y

instance Eq Char where
  x == y = predefinedeqchar x y

instance (Eq a) => Eq [a] where
  []      == []      = True
  (x:xs)  == []      = False
  []      == (y:ys)  = False
  (x:xs)  == (y:ys)  = x == y && xs == ys
```

FIGURE 1.1. **A type class for equality in HASKELL**

ent. Examples of proof assistants for functional languages are EVT [NFD01] for
ERLANG [AV91], SPARKLE [dMvEP01] for CLEAN [vEP01], and ERA [Win99]
for HASKELL [Jon03].

1.1.1 Type classes

A feature that is commonly found in functional programming languages is overloading structured by *type classes* [WB89]. Type classes essentially are groups
of types, the class *instances*, for which certain operations, the class *members*,
are implemented. These implementations are created from the available instance
definitions and may be different for each instance. The type of an instance definition is called the *instance head*. The equality operator will be used as a running
example throughout this paper (Figure 1.1).

In the most basic case, type classes have only one parameter and instance
heads are flat, that is, a single constructor applied to a list of type variables. Furthermore, no two instance definitions may overlap.

Several significant extensions have been proposed, such as multiple parameters [JJM97], overlapping instances, and instantiation with constructors [Jon93],
that have useful applications such as collections, coercion, isomorphisms and
mapping. In this paper, the term *general type classes* is used for systems of type
classes that support these extensions and non-flat instance heads. Figure 1.2 shows
a multi parameter class for the symmetric operation eq2.

An important observation regarding type classes is that, in general, the defined
instances should be semantically related. For example, all instances of the equality operator usually implement an equivalence relation. These properties can be
proven for all instances at once by proving them for the available instance definitions. Unfortunately, this is not straightforward because the instance definitions
may depend on each other and hence so will the proofs. For example, equality on

```
class Eq2 a b where
  eq2 :: a -> b -> Bool where

instance Eq2 Int Int where
  eq2 x y = x == y

instance Eq2 Char Char where
  eq2 x y = x == y

instance (Eq2 a b, Eq2 b c) => Eq2 (a, b) [c] where
  eq2 (x, y) [u, v] = eq2 x u && eq2 y v
  eq2 x y           = False

instance (Eq2 a b, Eq2 b c) => Eq2 [c] (a, b) where
  eq2 x y = eq2 y x
```

FIGURE 1.2.   A multi parameter class in HASKELL

lists is only symmetric if equality on the list members is so as well.

1.1.2   Contributions

The only proof assistant with special support for overloading that we know of is ISABELLE [Nip93, Wen97], which essentially supports single parameter type classes and a proof rule for it based on structural induction on types. However, we show that for general type classes, an effective tactic is not easily derived when structural induction is used. We use an induction scheme on types based on the instance definitions to solve this problem. Using this induction scheme, a proof rule and tactic are defined that are both strong enough and effective.

As a proof of concept, we have implemented the tactic in the proof assistant SPARKLE for the programming language CLEAN. The results, however, are generally applicable and can, for example, also be used for HASKELL and ISABELLE, if ISABELLE would support the specification of general type classes. In fact, the examples here are presented using HASKELL syntax. SPARKLE is dedicated to CLEAN, but can also be used to prove properties about HASKELL programs by translating them to CLEAN using the HACLE translator [Nay04].

1.1.3   Outline

The rest of this paper is structured as follows. First, the proof assistant SPARKLE is presented (Section 1.2). Then, basic definitions for instance definitions, evidence values, and class constrained properties are introduced (Section 1.3). After showing why structural induction does not suffice (Section 1.4), the proof rule and tactic based on the instance definitions are defined (Section 1.5) and extended to multiple class constraints (Section 1.6). We end with a discussion of the imple-

mentation (Section 1.7), related and future work (Section 1.8), and a summary of
the results (Section 1.9).

1.2 SPARKLE

The need for this work arose whilst improving the proof support for type classes
in SPARKLE. SPARKLE is a proof assistant specifically geared towards CLEAN,
which means that it can reason about CLEAN concepts using rules based on
CLEAN's semantics. Properties are specified in a first order predicate logic extended with equality on expressions. An example of this, using a slightly simplified syntax, is:

$$\textbf{example:}\ \forall_{n:\text{Int}|n\neq\perp}\forall_a\forall_{xs:[a]}[\texttt{take n xs ++ drop n xs = xs}]$$

These properties can be proven using *tactics*, which are user friendly operations
that transform a property into a number of logically stronger properties, the *proof
obligations* or *goals*, that are easier to prove. A tactic is the implementation of
(a combination of) theoretically sound *proof rules*. Whereas in general a proof
rule is theoretically simple but not very prover friendly, a tactic is prover friendly
but often theoretically more complex. The proof is complete when all remaining
proof obligations are trivial. Some useful tactics are, for example, reduction of
expressions, induction on expression variables, and rewriting using hypotheses.

In SPARKLE, properties that contain member functions can only be proven for
specific instances of that function. For example:

$$\textbf{sym}_{[\text{Int}]}\textbf{:}\ \forall_{x:[\text{Int}]}\forall_{y:[\text{Int}]}[\texttt{x == y} \rightarrow \texttt{y == x}]$$

can be easily proven by induction on lists using symmetry of equality on integers.
Proving that something holds for *all* instances, however, is not possible in general.
Consider for example symmetry of equality:

$$\textbf{sym:}\qquad \forall_a[\text{Eq} :: a \Rightarrow \forall_{x:a}\forall_{y:x}[\texttt{x == y} \rightarrow \texttt{y == x}]]$$

where Eq :: a denotes the, previously not available, constraint that equality must
be defined for type a. This property can be split into a property for every instance
definition, which gives among others the property for the instance for lists:

$$\textbf{sym}_{[a]}\textbf{:}\qquad \forall_a[\text{Eq} :: a \Rightarrow \forall_{x:[a]}\forall_{y:[a]}[\texttt{x == y} \rightarrow \texttt{y == x}]]$$

It is clear that this property is true as long as it is true for instance a. Unfortunately,
this hypothesis is not available. Using an approach based on induction, however,
we may be able to assume the hypotheses for all instances the instance definition
depends on, and hence will be able to prove the property.

Internally, SPARKLE translates type classes to *evidence values* or *dictionaries*
[WB89], that make the use of overloading explicit. The evidence value for a class

```
eqint ::  Int -> Int -> Bool
eqint = predefinedeqint

eqchar ::  Char -> Char -> Bool
eqchar = predefinedeqchar

eqlist ::  (a -> a -> Bool) -> ([a] -> [a] -> Bool)
eqlist ev []      []     = True
eqlist ev (x:xs)  []     = False
eqlist ev []      (y:ys) = False
eqlist ev (x:xs)  (y:ys) = ev x y && eqlist ev xs ys
```

FIGURE 1.3.   Translation of Figure 1.1

constraint c :: a is the evidence that there is an (implementation of the) instance of class c for type a. Hence, an evidence value exists if and only if the class constraint is satisfied. As usual, we will use the implementation itself as the evidence value. A program is translated by converting all instance definitions to functions (distinct names are created by suffixes). In expressions, the evidence value is substituted for member applications. When functions require certain classes to be defined, the evidence values for these constraints are passed as a parameter. Figure 1.3 shows an example of the result of the translation of the equality class from Figure 1.1.

1.3   PRELIMINARIES

Instead of defining a proof rule that operates on the example properties from Section 1.2, we define both instances and properties at the level that explicitly uses evidence values. In this section, basic definitions for instance definitions, evidence values, and class constrained properties are given.

1.3.1   Instance definitions

Because we intend to support constructor classes, types are formalized by a language of constructors [Jon93]:

$$\tau ::= \alpha \mid \chi \mid \tau\,\tau'$$

where α and χ range over a given set of type variables and type constructors respectively. For example, τ can be Int, [Int], and Tree Char, but also the [], Tree, and -> constructors that take types as an argument and yield a list, tree, or function type respectively. $TV(\tau)$ denotes the set of type variables occurring in τ. The set of closed types $\mathcal{T}^c$ is the set of types for which $TV(\tau)$ is empty.

Predicates are used to indicate that an instance of a certain class exists. An instance can be identified by an instantiation of the class parameters. The predicate

$c :: \bar{\tau}$ denotes that there is an instance of the class c for instantiation $\bar{\tau}$ of the class parameters. For example, Eq :: [Int] and Eq :: (Int, Int) denote that there is an instance of the Eq class for types [Int] and (Int, Int) respectively:

$$\pi ::= c :: \bar{\tau}$$

Because these predicates are used to constrain types to a certain class, they are called *class constraints*. Class constraints in which only type variables occur in the type, for example Eq :: a, are called *simple*. For reasons of simplicity, it is assumed that all type variables that occur in a class constraint are distinct.

Without loss of generality, throughout this paper we restrict ourselves to type classes that have only one member and no subclasses. Multiple members and subclasses can be supported using records of expressions for the evidence values. An instance definition:

$$\text{inst } \bar{\pi} \Rightarrow c :: \bar{\tau} = e$$

defines an instance $\bar{\tau}$ of class c for types that satisfy class constraints $\bar{\pi}$. The instance definition provides the translated expression e for the class member c. The functions $Head(\text{inst } c :: \bar{\pi} \Rightarrow \tau = e) = \tau$ and $Context(\text{inst } c :: \bar{\pi} \Rightarrow \tau = e) = \bar{\pi}$ will be used to retrieve the instance head and context respectively.

The program context ψ, that contains the function and class definitions, also includes the available instance definitions. The function $Idefs_\psi(c)$ returns the set of instance definitions of class c defined in program ψ.

1.3.2 Evidence values

From the translation from type classes to evidence values, as briefly summarized in Section 1.2, the rule for evidence creation is important for our purpose. Two definitions are required before it can be defined.

Firstly, because instance definitions are allowed to overlap, a mechanism is needed that chooses between them. Since the exact definition is not important for our purpose, we assume that the function $Ai_\psi(c :: \bar{\tau})$ determines the most specific instance definition applicable for instance $\bar{\tau}$ of class c. Ai_ψ is also defined for types that contain variables as long as it can be determined which instance definition should be applied.

Secondly, the *dependencies* of an instance are the instances it depends on:

$$Deps(c :: \bar{\tau}, i) = *_{Head(i) \to \bar{\tau}}(Context(i))$$

where $*_{\bar{\tau} \to \bar{\tau}'}$ denotes the substitutor that maps the type variables in $\bar{\tau}$ such that $*(\bar{\tau}) = \bar{\tau}'$. When i is not provided, $Ai_\psi(c :: \bar{\tau})$ is assumed for it.

Evidence values are now straightforwardly created by applying the expression of the most specific instance definition to the evidence values of its dependencies:

$$\frac{Deps(\pi) = \langle \pi_1, \ldots, \pi_n \rangle \qquad Ai_\psi(\pi) = \text{inst } c :: \bar{\pi}' \Rightarrow \bar{\tau}' = e}{Ev_\psi(\pi) = e \; Ev_\psi(\pi_1) \; \ldots \; Ev_\psi(\pi_n)}$$

In proofs, evidence values will be created assuming the evidence values for the dependencies are already assigned to expression variables:

$$\frac{Deps(\pi, i) = \langle \pi_1, \ldots, \pi_n \rangle \quad i = \mathsf{inst}\ c :: \bar{\pi}' \Rightarrow \bar{\tau}' = e}{Ev^p{}_\psi(\pi, i) = e\ \mathsf{ev}_{\pi_1}\ \ldots\ \mathsf{ev}_{\pi_n}}$$

assuming that the evidence for π is assigned to the variable ev_π. A specific instance definition i can be provided, because $Ai_\psi(\pi)$ might not be known in proofs.

1.3.3 Class constrained properties

In SPARKLE, properties are formalized by a first order predicate logic extended with equality on expressions. The equality on expressions is designed to handle infinite and undefined expressions well.

We extend these properties with class constraints, that can be used to constrain types to a certain class. These properties will be referred to as *class constrained properties*. For example, consider symmetry and transitivity of equality:

sym: $\quad \forall_a[\mathsf{Eq} :: a \Rightarrow \forall_{x, y:a}[\mathsf{ev}_{\mathsf{Eq}::a}\ x\ y \rightarrow \mathsf{ev}_{\mathsf{Eq}::a}\ y\ x]]$

trans: $\quad \forall_a[\mathsf{Eq} :: a \Rightarrow \forall_{x, y, z:a}[\mathsf{ev}_{\mathsf{Eq}::a}\ x\ y \rightarrow \mathsf{ev}_{\mathsf{Eq}::a}\ y\ z$
$\rightarrow \mathsf{ev}_{\mathsf{Eq}::a}\ x\ z]]$

The property $c :: \bar{\tau} \Rightarrow p$ means that in property p it is assumed that $\bar{\tau}$ is an instance of class c and the evidence value for this class constraint is assigned to $\mathsf{ev}_{c::\bar{\tau}}$. Thus, the semantics of the property $\pi \Rightarrow p$ is defined as $p_{[\mathsf{ev}_\pi \mapsto Ev_\psi(\pi)]}$.

1.4 STRUCTURAL INDUCTION

The approach for proving properties that contain overloaded identifiers taken in ISABELLE essentially is structural induction on types. In this section it is argued that the proof rule for general type classes should use another induction scheme.

Structural induction on types seems an effective approach because it gives more information about the type of an evidence value. This information can be used to expand evidence values. For example, $\mathsf{ev}_{\mathsf{Eq}::[a]}$ can be expanded to $\mathtt{eqlist}$ $\mathsf{ev}_{\mathsf{Eq}::a}$ (see Figure 1.3).

$$\frac{Ai_\psi(\pi) = i \quad \forall_{TV(\pi)}[Deps(\pi) \Rightarrow p(Ev^p{}_\psi(\pi))]}{\forall_{TV(\pi)}[\pi \Rightarrow p(\mathsf{ev}_\pi)]} \quad \textbf{(expand)}$$

More importantly, structural induction allows the property to be assumed for structurally smaller types. Ideally the hypothesis should be assumed for all dependencies on the same class. Unfortunately, structural induction does not always allow this for multi parameter classes.

Consider for example the multi parameter class in Figure 1.2. The instance of Eq2 for [Int] (Char, Char) depends on the instance for Char Int, which is not structurally smaller because Char is not structurally smaller than [Int], and Int is not structurally smaller than (Char, Char). Hence, the hypothesis cannot be assumed for this dependency. This problem can be solved by basing the induction scheme on the instance definitions.

1.5 INDUCTION ON INSTANCES

The induction scheme proposed in the previous section can be used on the set of defined instances of a class. In this section, a proof rule and tactic that use this scheme are defined and applied to some examples.

1.5.1 Proof rule and tactic

We first define the set of instances of a class and an order based on the instance definitions on it. The well-founded induction theorem applied to the defined set and order yields the proof rule. Then, the tactic is presented that can be derived from this rule.

Remember that the instances of a class are identified by sequences of closed types. $\bar{\tau}$ is an instance of class c if an evidence value can be generated for the class constraint $c :: \bar{\tau}$. Hence, the set of instances of class c can be defined as:

$$Inst_\psi(c) = \{\bar{\tau} \mid \forall_{c'::\bar{\tau}' \in Deps(c::\bar{\tau})}[\bar{\tau}' \in Inst_\psi(c')]\}$$

For example, $Inst_\psi(\texttt{Eq}) = \{\texttt{Int}, \texttt{Char}, \texttt{[Int]}, \texttt{[Char]}, \texttt{[[Int]]}, \ldots\}$.

An order on this set is straightforwardly defined. Because the idea is to base the order on the instance definitions, an instance $\bar{\tau}'$ is considered one step smaller than $\bar{\tau}$ if the evidence for $\bar{\tau}$ depends on the evidence for $\bar{\tau}'$, that is, if $c :: \bar{\tau}'$ is a dependency of the most specific instance definition for $c :: \bar{\tau}$. For example, Int $<^1_{(\psi,\texttt{Eq})}$ [Int] and [Char] $<^1_{(\psi,\texttt{Eq})}$ [[Char]].

$$\bar{\tau} <^1_{(\psi,c)} \bar{\tau}' \Leftrightarrow c :: \bar{\tau}' \in Deps(c :: \bar{\tau})$$

Note that there is a specific set of instances for each class and therefore also a specific order for each class.

Well-founded induction requires a well-founded partial order, for which we use the reflexive transitive closure of $<^1_{(\psi,c)}$. It can be easily derived from the way evidence values are generated that this is indeed a well-founded partial order. Applying this order, $\leqslant_{(\psi,c)}$, to the well-founded induction theorem yields the following proof rule:

$$\frac{\forall_{\bar{\tau} \in Inst_\psi(c)}[\forall_{\bar{\tau}' \leqslant_{(\psi,c)} \bar{\tau}}[p(\bar{\tau}')] \to p(\bar{\tau})]}{\forall_{\bar{\alpha} \in Inst_\psi(c)}[p(\bar{\alpha})]} \quad \textbf{(inst-rule)}$$

Rewriting the proof rule using the definitions of $Inst_\psi(c)$, $\leqslant_{(\psi,c)}$, evidence creation, and class constrained properties results in a tactic that can be directly applied to class constrained properties. For all class constraints $c :: \bar{\alpha}$:

$$
\frac{
\begin{array}{l}
\forall_{i \in Idefs_\psi(c)} \forall_{Head(i) \in \langle T^c \rangle} \\
\quad [\, Deps(c :: Head(i), i) \\
\quad\quad \Rightarrow \forall_{c' :: \bar{\tau}' \in Deps(c :: Head(i), i)} [c = c' \Rightarrow p(\mathrm{ev}_{c::\bar{\tau}'}, \bar{\tau}')] \\
\quad\quad \rightarrow p(Ev^p{}_\psi(c :: Head(i), i), Head(i)) \\
\quad]
\end{array}
}{
\forall_{\bar{\alpha} \in \langle T^c \rangle} [c :: \bar{\alpha} \Rightarrow p(\mathrm{ev}_{c::\bar{\alpha}}, \bar{\alpha})]
} \quad \textbf{(inst-tactic)}
$$

where it is assumed that all variables in $Head(i)$ are fresh. When the tactic is applied to a class constrained property, it generates a proof obligation for every available instance definition with hypotheses for all dependencies on the same class.

1.5.2 Results

The result is both a proof rule and a user friendly tactic. The tactic is nicely illustrated by symmetry of equality (Figure 1.1 and 1.3). When **(inst-tactic)** is applied to:

sym: $\quad \forall_a [Eq :: a \Rightarrow \forall_{x:a} \forall_{y:a} [\mathrm{ev}_{Eq::a} \; x \; y \rightarrow \mathrm{ev}_{Eq::a} \; y \; x]]$

it generates the following three proof obligations (one for each instance definition):

sym$_{\text{Int}}$: $\quad \forall_{x:\text{Int}} \forall_{y:\text{Int}} [\text{eqint} \; x \; y \rightarrow \text{eqint} \; y \; x]$

sym$_{\text{Char}}$: $\forall_{x:\text{Char}} \forall_{y:\text{Char}} [\text{eqchar} \; x \; y \rightarrow \text{eqchar} \; y \; x]$

sym$_{[a]}$: $\quad \forall_a \,[\, Eq :: a$
$\quad\quad \Rightarrow \forall_{x:a} \forall_{y:a} [\mathrm{ev}_{Eq::a} \; x \; y \rightarrow \mathrm{ev}_{Eq::a} \; y \; x]$
$\quad\quad \rightarrow \forall_{x:[a]} \forall_{y:[a]} [\text{eqlist} \; \mathrm{ev}_{Eq::a} \; x \; y \rightarrow \text{eqlist} \; \mathrm{ev}_{Eq::a} \; y \; x]$
$\quad]$

which are easily proven using the already available tactics.

The previous step could also have been taken using a tactic based on structural induction on types. However, **(inst-tactic)** can also assume hypotheses for dependencies that are possibly not structurally smaller. Consider for example the symmetry of eq2 in Figure 1.2:

sym2: $\quad \forall_{a,b} \,[\, Eq2 :: a \; b \Rightarrow Eq2 :: b \; a$
$\quad\quad \Rightarrow \forall_{x:a} \forall_{y:b} [\mathrm{ev}_{Eq2::a} \; b \; x \; y \rightarrow \mathrm{ev}_{Eq2::b} \; a \; y \; x]$
$\quad]$

Applying (**inst-tactic**) to this property generates a proof obligation for every instance definition, including one for the fourth instance of Eq2 in Figure 1.2, where eq2list is the translation of that instance definition:

$$
\textbf{sym2}_{[a]}\colon \quad \forall_{a,b,c}
$$
$$
\big[\, \text{Eq2} :: \text{b a} \Rightarrow \text{Eq2} :: \text{c a}
$$
$$
\Rightarrow \big[\text{Eq2} :: \text{a b} \Rightarrow \forall_{x:b}\forall_{y:a}\big[ev_{\text{Eq2}::b}\ \text{a}\ \text{x}\ \text{y} \rightarrow ev_{\text{Eq2}::a}\ \text{b}\ \text{y}\ \text{x}\big]\big]
$$
$$
\rightarrow \big[\text{Eq2} :: \text{a c} \Rightarrow \forall_{x:c}\forall_{y:a}\big[ev_{\text{Eq2}::c}\ \text{a}\ \text{x}\ \text{y} \rightarrow ev_{\text{Eq2}::a}\ \text{c}\ \text{y}\ \text{x}\big]\big]
$$
$$
\rightarrow \text{Eq2} :: (\text{b},\text{c})\ [\text{a}] \Rightarrow \forall_{x:[a]}\forall_{y:(b,c)}\big[
$$
$$
\text{eq2list}\ ev_{\text{Eq2}::b}\ \text{a}\ ev_{\text{Eq2}::c}\ \text{a}\ \text{x}\ \text{y}
$$
$$
\rightarrow ev_{\text{Eq2}::(b,c)\ [a]}\ \text{y}\ \text{x}\big]
$$
$$
\big]
$$

In this proof obligation, the hypotheses could not have been assumed when using structural induction on types (see Section 1.4), hence our tactic is useful in more cases.

1.6 MULTIPLE CLASS CONSTRAINTS

The proof rule and tactic presented in the previous section work well when the property has only one class constraint. In case of multiple class constraints, however, the rules might not be powerful enough. In this section it is shown that this problem does indeed occur. Therefore, a more general proof rule and tactic are defined and applied to some examples.

1.6.1 The problem

Consider the two class definitions in Figure 1.4. The translated instance definitions are respectively called fint, flist, ftree, gint, gtree, and glist at the level of dictionaries. Given the property:

$$
\textbf{same:} \quad \forall_a[f :: a \Rightarrow g :: a \Rightarrow [ev_{f::a}\ x = ev_{g::a}\ x]]
$$

Applying (**inst-tactic**) yields among others the goal:

$$
\textbf{same}_{[a]}\textbf{f:} \quad \forall_a[g :: [a] \Rightarrow \forall_{x:[a]}[\text{flist}\ ev_{g::a}\ x = ev_{g::a}\ x]]
$$

This goal has a non-simple class constraint, which can only be removed by evidence expansion (**expand**), resulting in:

$$
\textbf{same}_{[a]}\textbf{f':} \forall_a[f :: a \Rightarrow g :: a \Rightarrow \forall_{x:[a]}[\text{flist}\ ev_{g::a}\ x
$$
$$
= \text{glist}\ ev_{f::a}\ ev_{g::a}\ x]]
$$

After some reduction steps, this can be transformed into:

```
data Tree a = Leaf | Node a (Tree a) (Tree a)

class f a where f ::  a -> Bool

instance f Int where
  f x = x == x

instance (g a) => f [a] where
  f []     = True
  f (x:xs) = g x == g x

instance (f a, g a) => f (Tree a) where
  f Leaf          = True
  f (Node x l r) = f x == g x

class g a where g ::  a -> Bool

instance g Int where
  g x = x == x

instance (f a) => g (Tree a) where
  g Leaf          = True
  g (Node x l r) = f x == f x

instance (g a, f a) => g [a] where
  g []     = True
  g (x:xs) = g x == f x
```

FIGURE 1.4.   Problematic class definitions

$$\mathbf{same}_{[a]}\mathbf{f''}: \forall_a [f :: a \Rightarrow g :: a \Rightarrow \forall_{x:[a]}[ev_{g::a} \ x \ == \ ev_{g::a} \ x$$
$$= ev_{f::a} \ x \ == \ ev_{g::a} \ x]]$$

This proof obligation is true when $ev_{f::a} \ x = ev_{g::a} \ x$. Unfortunately, the induction scheme did not allow us to assume this hypothesis. Since this problem is caused by the fact that the type variables occur in more than one class constraint, the natural solution is to take multiple class constraints into account in the induction scheme.

1.6.2   Proof rule and tactic

We take the same approach as in the previous section. We first define the set of instances, the order, the proof rule and the tactic. Then, in Section 1.6.3, it is shown that the new tactic solves the problem.

First, the set of type sequences that are instances of all classes that occur in a list of class constraints is defined. $\bar{\tau}$ is a member of the set if all class constraints $\bar{\pi}$ are satisfied when all variables $TV(\bar{\pi})$ are replaced by the corresponding type from $\bar{\tau}$. We assume here that $TV(\bar{\pi})$ is a linearly ordered, for example lexicographically, sequence and that the elements of $\bar{\tau}$ are in the corresponding order. For example, $SetInst_\psi(\mathtt{f} :: \mathtt{a}, \mathtt{g} :: \mathtt{a}) = \{\mathtt{Int}, [\mathtt{Int}], \mathtt{Tree\ Int}, [[\mathtt{Int}]], \ldots\}$.

$$SetInst_\psi(\bar{\pi}) = \{\bar{\tau} \mid \forall_{c::\bar{\alpha}' \in \bar{\pi}}[*_{TV(\bar{\pi}) \to \bar{\tau}}(\bar{\alpha}') \in Inst_\psi(c)]\}$$

The order on this set is an extension of the order for single class constraints to sets. A sequence of types τ is considered one step smaller than τ' if $*_{TV(\pi) \to \tau}(\pi)$ is a subset of the dependencies of $*_{TV(\pi) \to \tau}(\pi)$. For example, $[\mathtt{Int}] <^1_{(\psi, \langle \mathtt{f}::\mathtt{a}, \mathtt{g}::\mathtt{a} \rangle)}$ $([[\mathtt{Int}]])$ because $\{\mathtt{f} :: [\mathtt{Int}], \mathtt{g} :: [\mathtt{Int}]\}$ is a subset of $Deps(\mathtt{g} :: [[\mathtt{Int}]]) \cup$ $Deps(\mathtt{f} :: [[\mathtt{Int}]])$. Here, sequences of class constraints are lifted to sets when required:

$$\bar{\tau} <^1_{\psi, \bar{\pi}} \tau' \Leftrightarrow *_{TV(\bar{\pi}) \to \bar{\tau}}(\bar{\pi}) \subseteq \bigcup_{\pi \in \bar{\pi}} [Deps(*_{TV(\bar{\pi}) \to \bar{\tau}'}(\pi))])$$

Again, it can be derived from the evidence creation that the reflexive transitive closure of this order, $\leqslant_{(\psi, \bar{\pi})}$, is a well-founded partial order.

Applying the well-founded induction theorem to this set and order yields the proof rule for multiple class constraints. For every sequence of simple class constraints $\bar{\pi}$:

$$\frac{\forall_{\bar{\tau} \in SetInst_\psi(\bar{\pi})} [\forall_{\bar{\tau}' \leqslant_{(\psi, \bar{\pi})} \bar{\tau}} [p(\bar{\tau}')] \to p(\bar{\tau})]}{\forall_{\bar{\tau} \in SetInst_\psi(\bar{\pi})} [p(\bar{\tau})]} \quad \textbf{(multi-rule)}$$

Because multiple class constraints are involved, defining the final tactic is a bit more complicated. Instead of all instance definitions, every combination of instance definitions, one for each class constraint, has to be tried. All of these instance definitions make assumptions about the types of the type variables, and these assumptions should be unifiable. Therefore, we define the most general unifier that takes the sharing of type variables across class constraints into account:

$$SetMgu(\langle c_1 :: \bar{\alpha}_1, \ldots, c_n :: \bar{\alpha}_n \rangle, \langle \tau_1, \ldots, \tau_n \rangle) = * \Leftrightarrow$$
$$\forall_{1 \leqslant i \leqslant n} [*(\bar{\alpha}_i) = \tau_i] \wedge \forall_{*'} [\forall_{1 \leqslant i \leqslant n} [*'(\bar{\alpha}_i) = \tau_i] \Rightarrow \exists *''[*' = *'' \circ *]]$$

Furthermore, for readability of the final tactic, some straightforward extensions of existing definitions to vectors are used:

$$
\begin{aligned}
Idefs_\psi(\langle \pi_1, \ldots, \pi_n \rangle) &= \{i_1, \ldots, i_n \mid i_j \in Idefs_\psi(\pi_j)\} \\
Head(\langle i_1, \ldots, i_n \rangle) &= \langle Head(i_1), \ldots, Head(i_n) \rangle \\
Ev^p{}_\psi(\langle \pi_1, \ldots, \pi_n \rangle, \langle i_1, \ldots, i_n \rangle) &= \langle Ev^p{}_\psi(\pi_1, i_1), \ldots, Ev^p{}_\psi(\pi_n, i_n) \rangle \\
ev_{\langle \pi_1, \ldots, \pi_n \rangle} &= \langle ev_{\pi_1}, \ldots, ev_{\pi_n} \rangle \\
Deps(\langle \pi_1, \ldots, \pi_n \rangle, \langle i_1, \ldots, i_n \rangle) &= \langle Deps(\pi_1, i_1), \ldots, Deps(\pi_n, i_n) \rangle
\end{aligned}
$$

Finally, using the presented definitions, evidence creation, class constrained properties, and the proof rule, the tactic can be defined. For every sequence of simple class constraints $\bar{\pi}$:

$$
\frac{
\begin{array}{l}
\forall_{\bar{\imath}\in Idefs_{\psi}(\bar{\pi})} \exists_{*|*=SetMgu(\bar{\pi},Head(\bar{\imath}))} \forall_{*(Head(\bar{\imath}))\in\langle\mathcal{T}^c\rangle} \\
\quad [\, Deps(*(\bar{\pi}),\bar{\imath}) \\
\qquad \Rightarrow \forall_{*'|*'(\bar{\pi})\subseteq Deps(*(\bar{\pi}),\bar{\imath})}[p(\mathrm{ev}_{*'(\bar{\pi})},*'(TV(\bar{\pi})))] \\
\qquad \rightarrow p(Ev^p{}_{\psi}(*(\bar{\pi}),\bar{\imath}),*(Head(\bar{\imath}))) \\
\quad]
\end{array}
}{
\forall_{TV(\bar{\pi})}[\bar{\pi}\Rightarrow p(\mathrm{ev}_{\bar{\pi}},TV(\bar{\pi}))]
} \quad \textbf{(multi-tactic)}
$$

Note that applying this tactic may result in non-simple class constraints when non-flat instance types are used. For non-simple class constraints, the induction tactics cannot be applied, but the **(expand)** rule might be used. However, in practice most instance definitions will have flat types.

This solution for multiple class constraints has some parallels to the constraint set satisfiability problem (CS-SAT), the problem of determining if there are types that satisfy a set of class constraints. The general CS-SAT problem is undecidable. However, recently, an algorithm was proposed [CFV04] that essentially tries to create a type that satisfies all constraints by trying all combinations of instance definitions, as we have been doing in our tactic.

1.6.3 Results

In this section, we have generalized the proof rule and tactic from Section 1.5 to multiple class constraints. In case of a single class constraint, the new rules behave exactly the same as **(inst-rule)** and **(inst-tactic)**. However, now we can apply **(multi-tactic)** to multiple class constraints at once. Given the previously problematic property:

same: $\quad \forall_a[f :: a \Rightarrow g :: a \Rightarrow [\mathrm{ev}_{f::a}\ x = \mathrm{ev}_{g::a}\ x]]$

this yields three proof obligations, one for every unifiable combination of instance definitions:

same$_{\mathrm{Int}}$: $\quad \forall_a[\texttt{fint}\ x = \texttt{gint}\ x]$

same$_{[a]}$: $\quad \forall_a[f :: a \Rightarrow g :: a \Rightarrow \forall_{x:a}[\mathrm{ev}_{f::a}\ x = \mathrm{ev}_{g::a}\ x]$
$\qquad\qquad \rightarrow \forall_{x:[a]}[\texttt{flist}\ \mathrm{ev}_{g::a}\ x = \texttt{glist}\ \mathrm{ev}_{f::a}\ \mathrm{ev}_{g::a}\ x]]$

same$_{\mathrm{Tree\ a}}$:$\forall_a[f :: a \Rightarrow g :: a \Rightarrow \forall_{x:a}[\mathrm{ev}_{f::a}\ x = \mathrm{ev}_{g::a}\ x]$
$\qquad\qquad \rightarrow \forall_{x:\mathrm{Tree\ a}}[\texttt{ftree}\ \mathrm{ev}_{f::a}\ \mathrm{ev}_{g::a}\ x = \texttt{gtree}\ \mathrm{ev}_{g::a}\ x]$

The goal **same$_{[a]}$** (and **same$_{\mathrm{Tree\ a}}$**) now has a hypothesis that can be used to prove the goal using the already available tactics. Hence, by taking multiple class constraints into account the problem is solved.

1.7 IMPLEMENTATION

As a proof of concept, we have implemented the (**multi-tactic**) tactic extended
for multiple members and subclasses in SPARKLE. Because of the similarity to
the already available induction tactic and the clearness of the code, the implementation of the tactic took very little time. However, to implement the tactic, the
typing rules had to be extended. The translation of type classes to dictionaries is
only typeable in general using rank-2 polymorphism, which is currently not supported by SPARKLE. This was worked around by handling the dictionary creation
and selection in a way that hides the rank-2 polymorphism. Ideally, the use of
dictionaries should be completely hidden from the user as well.

The tactic has been used to prove, amongst others, the examples in this paper.
The implementation is available at:

`http://www.student.kun.nl/ronvankesteren/SparkleGTC.zip`

1.8 RELATED AND FUTURE WORK

As mentioned in Section 1.1, the general proof assistant ISABELLE [NPW02] supports overloading and single parameter type classes. ISABELLE's notion of type
classes is somewhat different from HASKELL's in that it represents types that satisfy certain properties instead of types for which certain values are defined. Nevertheless, the problems to be solved are equivalent. ISABELLE [Nip93, Wen97]
uses a proof rule based on structural induction on types, which suffices for the
supported type classes. However, if ISABELLE would support more extensions,
most importantly multi parameter classes, it would be useful to define our proof
rule and a corresponding tactic in ISABELLE.

Essentially, the implementation of the tactic we proposed extends the induction techniques available in SPARKLE. Leonard Lensink proposed and implemented extensions of SPARKLE for induction and co-induction for mutually recursive functions and data types [LvE04]. The main goal was to ease proofs by
making the induction scheme match the structure of the program. Together with
this work this significantly increases the applicability of SPARKLE.

Because generics is often presented as an extension of type classes [HJ00],
it would be nice to extend this work to generics as well. Currently, in CLEAN
generics are translated to normal type classes where classes are created for every
available data type [AP01]. There is a library for HASKELL that generates classes
with boilerplate code for every available data type [LJ03]. The tactic presented
here can already be used to prove properties about generic functions by working
on these generated type classes. However, the property is only proven for the
data types that are used in the program and a separate proof is required for each
data type. That is, after all, the main difference between normal type classes and
generics. Hence, it remains useful to define a proof rule specifically for generics.

1.9 CONCLUSION

In this paper, we have presented a proof rule for class constrained properties and an effective tactic based on it. Although structural induction on types is theoretically powerful enough, we showed that for an effective tactic an induction scheme should be used that is based on the instance definitions. The tactic is effective, because, using the defined proof rule, it allows all sensible hypotheses to be assumed. The rule and tactic were first defined for single class constraints and then generalized to properties with multiple class constraints.

As a proof of concept, the resulting tactic is implemented in SPARKLE for the programming language CLEAN, but it can also be used for proving properties about HASKELL programs. This is, to our knowledge, the first implementation of an effective tactic for general type classes. If ISABELLE would support extensions for type classes, the tactic could be implemented in ISABELLE as well.

Acknowledgements.   We would like to thank Sjaak Smetsers for his suggestions and advice concerning this work, especially on the semantics of type classes in CLEAN, and Fermín Reig for a valuable discussion on generic proofs at the TFP2004 workshop.

REFERENCES

[AP01]   A. Alimarine and R. Plasmeijer. A generic programming extension for Clean. In Th. Arts and M. Mohnen, editors, *Proceedings of the 13th International Workshop on the Implementation of Functional Languages, IFL 2001, Selected Papers*, LNCS 2312, pages 168–185, Älvsjö, Sweden, September 24-26 2001. Springer, Berlin.

[AV91]   J. L. Armstrong and R. Virding.   Erlang – An Experimental Telephony Switching Language. In *XIII International Switching Symposium*, Stockholm, Sweden, May 27 – June 1, 1991.

[CFV04]   C. Camarão, L. Figueiredo, and C. Vasconcellos. Constraint-set satisfiability for overloading. In *International Conference on Principles and Practice of Declarative Programming*, Verona, Italy, August 2004.

[dMvEP01] M. de Mol, M. van Eekelen, and R. Plasmeijer. Theorem proving for functional programmers - SPARKLE: A functional theorem prover. In Th. Arts and M. Mohnen, editors, *Proceedings of the 13th International Workshop on the Implementation of Functional Languages, IFL 2001, Selected Papers*, LNCS 2312, pages 55–71, Älvsjö, Sweden, September 2001.

[dt04]   The Coq development team. *The Coq proof assistant reference manual (version 8.0)*. LogiCal Project, 2004.

[HJ00]   R. Hinze and S. Peyton Jones. Derivable type classes. In G. Hutton, editor, *Proceedings of the 2000 ACM SIGPLAN Haskell Workshop*, volume 41(1):5–35 of *Electronic Notes in Theoretical Computer Science*. Elsevier Science, 2000.

[JJM97]   S. Peyton Jones, M. Jones, and E. Meijer. Type classes: an exploration of the
             design space. In *Proceedings of the Second Haskell Workshop*, Amsterdam,
             June 1997.

[Jon93]   M. Jones. A system of constructor classes: overloading and implicit higher-
             order polymorphism. In *FPCA '93: Conference on Functional Programming
             and Computer Architecture, Copenhagen, Denmark*, pages 52–61, 1993.
             ACM Press, New York.

[Jon03]   S. Peyton Jones. *Haskell 98 Language and Libraries*. Cambridge University
             Press, 2003.

[LJ03]   R. Lämmel and S. Jones. Scrap your boilerplate: A practical design pat-
             tern for generic programming. In *ACM SIGPLAN International Workshop
             on Types in Language Design and Implementation (TLDI'03)*, pages 26–37,
             New Orleans, January 2003. ACM Press, New York.

[LvE04]   L. Lensink and M. van Eekelen. Induction and Co-induction in Sparkle. In
             Hans-Wolfgang Loidl, editor, *Fifth Symposium on Trends in Functional Pro-
             gramming (TFP 2004)*, pages 273–293. Ludwig-Maximilians Universität,
             München, November 2004. Intellect, Bristol.

[Nay04]   M. Naylor. Haskell to Clean translation. University of York, 2004.

[NFD01]   T. Noll, L. Fredlund, and D.Gurov. The EVT Erlang verification tool. In
             *Proceedings of the 7th international Conference on Tools and Algorithms for
             the Construction and Analysis of Systems (TACAS'01)*, LNCS 2031, pages
             582–585, Stockholm, 2001. Springer, Berlin.

[Nip93]   T. Nipkow. Order-sorted polymorphism in Isabelle. In Gérard Huet and
             Gordon Plotkin, editors, *Logical Environments*, pages 164–188. CUP, 1993.

[NPW02]   T. Nipkow, L. C. Paulson, and M. Wenzel. *Isabelle/HOL — A Proof Assistant
             for Higher-Order Logic*. LNCS 2283. Springer, Berlin, 2002.

[OSRSC99]   S. Owre, N. Shankar, J. M. Rushby, and D. W. J. Stringer-Calvert. *PVS Lan-
             guage Reference*. Computer Science Laboratory, SRI International, Menlo
             Park, CA, September 1999.

[vEP01]   M. van Eekelen and R. Plasmeijer. *Concurrent Clean Language Report (ver-
             sion 2.0)*. University of Nijmegen, December 2001.

[WB89]   P. Wadler and S. Blott. How to make ad-hoc polymorphism less ad-hoc.
             In *Conference Record of the 16th Annual ACM Symposium on Principles
             of Programming Languages*, pages 60–76. ACM Press, New York, January
             1989.

[Wen97]   M. Wenzel. Type classes and overloading in higher-order logic. In E. Gunter
             and A. Felty, editors, *Proceedings of the 10th International Conference on
             Theorem Proving in Higher Order Logics (TPHOLs'97)*, LNCS 1275, pages
             307–322, Murray Hill, New Jersey, 1997. Springer, Berlin.

[Win99]   N. Winstanley. *Era User Manual (version 2.0)*. University of Glasgow, 1999.

Chapter 2

Generic Proofs for Combinator-based Generic Programs

Fermín Reig[1]

Abstract: Generic programming can bring important benefits to software engineering. In particular, it reduces the burden of verification, since generic proofs can be instantiated at many types. Reasoning about programs that use type classes does not enjoy the benefits of generic reasoning, as it requires providing proofs for an arbitrary number of type instances. This makes the process very impractical. We describe a useful method to reason about a class of programs that use type classes, based on the idea that generic functions implemented using overloading can also be expressed polytypically. We demonstrate the method on functions from the 'scrap-your-boilerplate' library, a collection of combinators for generic programming that has been proposed and implemented recently.

2.1 INTRODUCTION

Generic programming enables concise definitions of functions over many types. In the case of parametric polymorphism, the code of the function is the same at every type. In the case of polytypism, the code is different at each type, but it can be derived mechanically from a single polytypic definition [JJ96, Hin00a].

If similar functions have to be written over and over again for many types, then source code becomes larger. Programming errors increase with program size, and so does the cost of verifying, maintaining and documenting code. Two important benefits of generic programming are smaller programs and smaller proofs.

A number of systems for generic programming have been developed recently [JJ96, Hin00b, AP01, NJ04, LPJ03]. In Generic Haskell [Hin00b], generic func-

---

[1]School of Computer Science and I.T., University of Nottingham.

tions are defined by induction on the structure of types. To define a generic function, the programmer provides cases for basic types and for structured types built from sums and products. From this information, a compiler or specialiser can generate instances of the generic function for arbitrary types. Here is an example:

$$
\begin{array}{ll}
add\langle Bool\rangle & = (\vee) \\
add\langle Int\rangle & = (+) \\
add\langle A \times B\rangle\ (x,y)\ \ (x',y') & = (add\langle A\rangle\ x\ x', add\langle B\rangle\ y\ y') \\
add\langle A + B\rangle\ (inl\ x)\ (inl\ y) & = inl\ (add\langle A\rangle\ x\ y) \\
add\langle A + B\rangle\ (inr\ x)\ (inr\ y) & = inr\ (add\langle B\rangle\ x\ y) \\
add\langle A + B\rangle\ \_\ \ \ \ \ \_ & = error\ \texttt{"shape mismatch"}
\end{array}
$$

This function does point-wise addition of two structures (lists, trees, matrices,...) of the same type and shape. The structures may contain booleans and integers. This style of generic programming has been implemented in Generic Haskell and in Clean [AP01]. Because generic functions take types as parameters in this style, they are also called type-indexed functions. Another proposal, the 'scrap-your-boilerplate' library ([LPJ03] [LPJ03, LPJ04]), provides a collection of combinators for traversing values of arbitrary datatypes, together with combinators to simulate dynamic type case. A function similar to the one given above can be written like this:

$$
add\ x\ y = gzipWith\ ((mkTT\ (+)\ `extTT`\ (mkTT\ (\vee))))\ x\ y
$$

Here, *gzipWith* pairs matching values in x and y, and fails if the shapes are different. Then, a dynamic type check on matching values is performed, followed by 'or', addition, or failure if the corresponding types are respectively both boolean, both integer, or something else.

The two approaches support different styles of generic programming and are not comparable in terms of the class of generic functions that can be defined.

Little is known about the formal properties of the 'boilerplate' combinators. [LPJ03] state the following laws about the combinators *gmapT* and *gmapQ*:

$$
\begin{array}{ll}
gmapT\ id & = id \\
(gmapT\ t)\ \circ (gmapT\ t') & = gmapT\ (t\ \circ t') \\
(gmapQ\ q)\circ (gmapT\ t) & = gmapQ\ (q\circ t)
\end{array}
$$

However, no proofs are provided in that paper. Using the methods proposed by [Pau04] and [vvd05], it would be possible to prove these laws for a large number of types. Unfortunately, this methodology does not scale too well, since a new proof is required when we consider an additional base type or type constructor. What we really need are *generic* proofs that cover all possible types.

One of the contributions of this paper is to give generic proofs of the above laws. [LPJ03] use Haskell type classes to define traversal combinators. Our insight is that *gmapT* and *gmapQ* can be defined polytypically instead. We implement them in Generic Haskell, which supports proofs about generic functions (by induction on the structure of the type cases) [Hin00a].

A programmer might reasonably expect that similar fusion laws hold for the 'boilerplate' combinators that generalise *gmapT* and *gmapQ*. Another contribution of this paper is to show that this is not the case, perhaps contrary to programmers' intuition. We also *calculate* conditions that tell us when fusion can be applied to traversals using the more general combinators. This result can be used (by programmers or compilers) to transform code for improved efficiency. To our knowledge, this represents the first published account of formal reasoning about programs that use the 'boilerplate' combinators.

2.2 'BOILERPLATE' COMBINATORS AS GENERIC FUNCTIONS

The 'boilerplate' library is of help when writing programs that do traversals of data built from elaborate, mutually-recursive types. By using a few simple combinators, programmers can avoid writing most of the traversal code by hand. The approach is based on basic combinators that implement one-level, non-recursive traversals. From them, it is possible to implement more complex traversals, such as exhaustive top-down or bottom-up traversal. There are combinators for transforming values and for querying them; and there are purely functional and monadic versions of the combinators.

The basic combinators are *gmapT*, which applies a generic transformation to the top-level children of a value, and *gmapQ*, which applies a generic query to the top-level children of a value and returns a list of the results. For instance, let x be the value $('a', ('b', 'c'))$ and t the transformation that converts characters to upper case and is the identity transformation at any other type. Then $gmapT\ t\ x$ evaluates to $('A', ('b', 'c'))$. That is, the mapping is not recursive (x has two top-level children, $'a'$ and the pair $('b', 'c')$; t is the identity on pairs). Let q be the query that gets the ASCII number of a character and returns -1 for any other type. Then $gmapQ\ q\ x$ evaluates to the list $[97, -1]$.

Because of the regularity of their behaviour, instances of *gmapT* and *gmapQ* can be generated automatically for every type.[2] Alternatively, *gmapT* and *gmapQ* can be defined as generic functions. By doing so, we gain the possibility of using existing reasoning principles for generic programs [Hin00a]. Here is a polytypic implementation of *gmapT*. Later in the paper, we will use this version to prove the equivalence $(gmapT\ t) \circ (gmapT\ t') = gmapT\ (t \circ t')$.

$$
\begin{array}{lll}
gmapT\langle 0 \rangle & \_\,b & = b \\
gmapT\langle Unit \rangle & \_\,u & = u \\
gmapT\langle Int \rangle & \_\,i & = i \\
gmapT\langle A + B \rangle & t\ (inl\ l) & = inl\ (gmapT\langle A \rangle\ t\ l) \\
gmapT\langle A + B \rangle & t\ (inr\ r) & = inr\ (gmapT\langle B \rangle\ t\ r) \\
gmapT\langle A_1 \times \cdots \times A_n \rangle\ t\ (x_1, ..., x_n) & = (t\langle A_1 \rangle\ x_1,\ ...,\ t\langle A_n \rangle\ x_n)
\end{array}
$$

Here, 0 is the empty type, whose only value is $\bot$. It is sometimes useful to

---

[2]In the current implementation, the combinator *gfoldl* is generated, and *gmapT* and *gmapQ* are defined in terms of it [LPJ04].

define a datatype with a component of type 0 [Lö04]. In this paper we make use of the case for 0 in some of the proofs. Two comments about this definition of *gmapT* are in order. First, note that *t*, the first argument to *gmapT*, is itself a generic function: it is applied at different types $(A_1, \ldots, A_n)$ in the last equation. Not all implementations of polytypism support first-class generic functions. Hinze's recent version, based on type classes [Hin04], allows them, since generic functions are ordinary Haskell functions.[3] On the other hand, implementations based on translation by specialisation do not support them, although it is the topic of current research [Lö04]. Second, in languages like Generic Haskell, generic functions are defined by providing type cases for binary sums and products, but we have written a case for *n*-ary products (using an ellipsis as informal syntax). Supporting *n*-ary products in Generic Haskell raises technical difficulties with the types and implementation of generic functions. Fortunately, it is possible to avoid *n*-ary products if we translate our definitions to Generic Haskell extended with views [HJL05]. The code for *gmapT* would be almost identical; only the last line would need to be changed to the following:

$$gmapT\langle A \times B \rangle \ t \ (x, y) = (gmapT\langle A \rangle \ t \ x, \ t\langle B \rangle \ y)$$

In this paper, though, we prefer to use *n*-ary products, since the resulting definitions correspond more naturally to the English description of the behaviour, namely 'apply to all top-level children'. If we used the alternative definition using views and binary products, our proofs would require only minor changes, just like the code. Here is our polytypic implementation of *gmapQ*.

$$
\begin{array}{llll}
gmapQ\langle 0 \rangle & - & = [\,] \\
gmapQ\langle Unit \rangle & - & = [\,] \\
gmapQ\langle Int \rangle & - & = [\,] \\
gmapQ\langle A + B \rangle & q \ (inl \ l) & = gmapQ\langle A \rangle \ q \ l \\
gmapQ\langle A + B \rangle & q \ (inr \ r) & = gmapQ\langle B \rangle \ q \ r \\
gmapQ\langle A_1 \times \cdots \times A_n \rangle \ q \ (x_1, \ldots, x_n) & = [q\langle A_1 \rangle \ x_1, \ \ldots, \ q\langle A_n \rangle \ x_n]
\end{array}
$$

Later in the paper, we will use this definition to prove the equivalence

$$(gmapQ \ q) \circ (gmapT \ t) = gmapQ \ (q \circ t).$$

2.3 GENERIC PROOFS FOR 'BOILERPLATE' COMBINATORS

Generic functions are defined by induction on the structural representation of types. A suitable proof method for such definitions is fixed-point induction [Hin00a]. The main advantage of these proofs is that they are generic, in the sense that a single, type-indexed proof covers all its type instantiations. To construct a proof of

---

[3]In fact, [Hin04] uses Haskell98. First-class generic functions require rank-2 polymorphism, which is not Haskell98. However, popular Haskell implementations support this extension.

a predicate P about generic functions, we first write it as a type-indexed predicate $P\langle T\rangle$. Then, we need to show that it holds for the empty type, for basic types, and that it is preserved by type constructors:

$$P\langle 0\rangle$$
$$P\langle Unit\rangle$$
$$P\langle Int\rangle$$
$$\forall A\, B.P\langle A\rangle \,\wedge P\langle B\rangle \,\Rightarrow P\langle A+B\rangle$$
$$\forall A_1 \ldots A_n.P\langle A_1\rangle \,\wedge \ldots \wedge P\langle A_n\rangle \,\Rightarrow P\langle A_1 \times \cdots \times A_n\rangle$$

Fixed-point induction is applicable if P is an inclusive predicate, i.e. it can be written as a universally quantified conjunction of disjunctions [Sch86]. All the predicates that are proved using fixed-point induction in this paper are inclusive.

2.4   A PROOF OF THE FUSION LAW FOR *gmapT*

The fusion law for *gmapT* says that two consecutive one-level traversals can be fused into one.

Theorem 2.1. $\langle \forall t\, t' \;::\; (gmapT\, t) \circ (gmapT\, t') = gmapT\, (t \circ t')\rangle$

This law allows a program transformation that reduces the number of traversals over a data structure. We prepare for the proof by stating the fusion law as a type-indexed predicate, with explicit type parameters in applications of generic functions:

$$P\langle T\rangle \;= \langle \forall t\, t' \;::\; (gmapT\langle T\rangle\, t) \circ (gmapT\langle T\rangle\, t') = gmapT\langle T\rangle\, (t \circ t')\rangle$$

We now have to show that $P\langle T\rangle$ holds for all possible types T. The base case are the empty type and the primitive types.
- **Case $T = 0\,/\,Unit\,/\,Int$**

$$gmapT\langle T\rangle\, t\, (gmapT\langle T\rangle\, t'\, x)$$
$$= \quad \{\text{ definition of } gmapT\langle 0\,/\,Unit\,/\,Int\rangle \;\}$$
$$gmapT\langle T\rangle\, t\, x$$
$$= \quad \{\text{ definition of } gmapT\langle 0\,/\,Unit\,/\,Int\rangle \;\}$$
$$x$$
$$= \quad \{\text{ definition of } gmapT\langle 0\,/\,Unit\,/\,Int\rangle \;\}$$
$$gmapT\langle T\rangle\, (t \circ t')\, x$$

The induction steps are sums and products. For sums, we need to invoke the induction hypothesis. We only show the case for *inl*; the case for *inr* is symmetric.
- **Case $T = A + B, x = inl\, a$**

$$gmapT\langle T\rangle\, t\, (gmapT\langle T\rangle\, t'\, x)$$

$$= \quad \{ \text{ definition of } gmapT\langle A+B\rangle , x = inl\ a \}$$
$$gmapT\langle T\rangle\ t\ (inl\ (gmapT\langle A\rangle\ t'\ a))$$
$$= \quad \{ \text{ definition of } gmapT\langle A+B\rangle \}$$
$$inl\ (gmapT\langle A\rangle\ t\ (gmapT\langle A\rangle\ t'\ a))$$
$$= \quad \{ \text{ induction } \}$$
$$inl\ (gmapT\langle A\rangle\ (t\circ t')\ a)$$
$$= \quad \{ \text{ definition of } gmapT\langle A+B\rangle , x = inl\ a \}$$
$$gmapT\langle T\rangle\ (t\circ t')\ x$$

For tuples, we don't even need the induction hypothesis; we only make use of the definitions of $gmapT$ and the function composition operator.

• **Case** $T = A_1 \times \cdots \times A_n, x = (x_1,...,x_n)$

$$gmapT\langle T\rangle\ t\ (gmapT\langle T\rangle\ t'\ x)$$
$$= \quad \{ \text{ definition of } gmapT\langle A_1 \times \cdots \times A_n\rangle \}$$
$$gmapT\langle T\rangle\ t\ (t'\langle A_1\rangle\ x_1,\ ...,\ t'\langle A_n\rangle\ x_n)$$
$$= \quad \{ \text{ definition of } gmapT\langle A_1 \times \cdots \times A_n\rangle ; \text{ function composition } \}$$
$$((t\circ t')\langle A_1\rangle\ x_1,\ ...,\ (t\circ t')\langle A_n\rangle\ x_n)$$
$$= \quad \{ \text{ definition of } gmapT\langle A_1 \times \cdots \times A_n\rangle \}$$
$$gmapT\langle T\rangle\ (t\circ t')\ x$$

The other fusion theorem says that a one-level traversal followed by a one-level query can be fused into a one-level query.

Theorem 2.2. $\langle \forall q\ t\ ::\ (gmapQ\ q)\circ(gmapT\ t) = gmapQ\ (q\circ t)\rangle$

The proof proceeds in a similar way to the one shown above. It is included in the full version of the paper [Rei05]. We omit the proof of $gmapT\ id = id$, since it is similar to these two.

In the next section, we give a function over lists and a theorem about that function. We then generalise to a generic function over arbitrary types, and a corresponding theorem. Finally, we construct a generic proof of the theorem.

2.5   A THEOREM ABOUT *occurs*

Consider the following polymorphic function that counts the number of occurrences of a value in a list:

$$occursList \in (Eq\ a) \Rightarrow a \to [a] \to Int$$
$$occursList\ v = length \circ filter\ (\equiv v)$$

This performs two list traversals. A version that makes only one is easy to write, but the one shown here is slightly more concise; consider it a specification, but one that is executable. This function satisfies the following theorem:

Theorem 2.3. $\langle \forall x \; xs \; f \; :: \; occursList \; x \; xs \; \leqslant \; occursList \; (f \; x) \; (map \; f \; xs) \rangle$

Similar functions for other data structures, such as trees, are likely to be useful as part of a complete library. For each of them we would also state a similar theorem. Even better is to write a single generic function, state a single theorem, and write one proof only. Here is such a generic function, implemented with the 'boilerplate' combinators.

$$occurs \; x \; xs = everything \; (+) \; (0 \; `mkQ` \; cnt) \; xs$$
$$\textbf{where}$$
$$cnt \; y = \textbf{if} \; y \equiv x \; \textbf{then} \; 1 \; \textbf{else} \; 0$$

This traverses every node of xs, produces an integer for each one of them, and adds them all together. We describe the code briefly, but refer the reader to [LPJ03] for the details of the combinators $everything$ and mkQ. The combinator mkQ turns functions into generic queries that can be applied to arguments of any type. If a node n has the same type as x, then cnt is applied to n; otherwise, the default value 0 is returned. The function $everything$ is defined as follows: $everything \; k \; q \; x = foldl \; k \; (q \; x) \; (gmapQ \; (everything \; k \; q) \; x)$

A generic theorem

The theorem that the generic function satisfies is the following:

Theorem 2.4.
$$\langle \forall x \; xs \; f \; :: \; fusable \; (f) \; \Rightarrow \; occurs \; x \; xs \; \leqslant \; occurs \; (f \; x) \; (everywhere \; (mkT \; f) \; xs) \rangle$$

The function $everywhere$ traverses values bottom-up. Here, it applies the generic transformation $(mkT \; f)$ to every node of xs, bottom-up. Its definition is:

$$everywhere \; t = t \circ gmapT \; (everywhere \; t)$$

The combinator mkT makes a generic transformation from a function, that is, it extends the function to arguments of any type. Its specification is:

$$(mkT \; f) \; x = f \; x, \; \text{if the type of } x \text{ is the same as the domain of } f$$
$$(mkT \; f) \; x = x \; \; , \; \text{otherwise}$$

The predicate $fusable$ says that an $everywhere$ transformation followed by an $everything$ query, can be performed as a single traversal:

$$fusable \; (f) = \langle \forall xs \; q \; :: \; everything \; (+) \; q \; (everywhere \; (mkT \; f) \; xs) = $$
$$everything \; (+) \; (q \circ (mkT \; f)) \; xs \rangle$$

This generalises Theorem 2.2 from one-level traversals to full bottom-up traversals. We believe (but have not proved yet) that this predicate is satisfied for transformations that do not alter the shape of the value xs.

The reader may wonder why the generic theorem includes this condition, making it weaker than the specific theorem about lists. The 'boilerplate' implementation of *occurs* is more general and can be used to count occurrences of a value x of type a, not only in a container of as, but in a structure of arbitrary type. In general, an *everywhere* transformation is more general than *map* over a container type. For instance, the transformation can remove elements from a container, which *map* is guaranteed not to do. These more general functions satisfy weaker properties.

A generic proof

Our first attempt at a generic proof resulted in a long, complex proof by induction on types. Just like large programs, long proofs written by hand are more likely to contain errors. Subsequently, we managed to produce a concise proof where only a few lemmas require proofs by induction on types. In the proof, we use a version of the code where the function *cnt* has been lambda-lifted because having x as a free variable in *cnt* complicates things.

$$occurs\ x\ xs = everything\ (+)\ (q\ x)\ xs$$
$$\textbf{where}$$
$$q\ x = (0\ `mkQ`\ (cnt\ x))$$
$$cnt\ x = \lambda y \rightarrow \textbf{if}\ x \equiv y\ \textbf{then}\ 1\ \textbf{else}\ 0$$

We make use of a number of lemmas. The first two say that *gmapQ* and *everything* preserve ordering.

Lemma 2.1. $\langle \forall q\ q'\ ::\ q\ \dot{\leqslant}\ q'\ \Rightarrow\ gmapQ\ q\ \dot{\leqslant}\ gmapQ\ q' \rangle$

Lemma 2.2. $\langle \forall q\ q'\ ::\ q\ \dot{\leqslant}\ q'\ \Rightarrow\ everything\ (+)\ q\ \dot{\leqslant}\ everything\ (+)\ q' \rangle$

We use the symbol $\dot{\leqslant}$ to denote point-wise ordering between functions: $f\ \dot{\leqslant}\ g = \langle \forall x\ ::\ f\ x\ \leqslant\ g\ x \rangle$. When xs and ys are lists, we say that $xs \leqslant ys$ if they have the same length and corresponding elements are related by $\leqslant$.

For conciseness, we define the following shorthand. $q'\ f\ x = (q\ (f\ x)) \circ (mkT\ f)$, where q is the query from the **where** clause in the definition of *occurs*. It is used in our last lemma.

Lemma 2.3. $\langle \forall x f\ ::\ q\ x\ \dot{\leqslant}\ q'\ f\ x \rangle$

Proofs of the lemmas are included in an appendix. Finally, with the help of all this, we can give an equational proof of Theorem 2.4 that is simple and short.

$occurs \; x \; xs$

$= \quad \{ \text{ definition of } occurs \; \}$

$\quad everything \; (+) \; (q \; x) \; xs$

$= \quad \{ \text{ definition of } everything \; \}$

$\quad foldl \; (+) \; (q \; x \; xs) \; (gmapQ \; (everything \; (+) \; (q \; x)) \; xs)$

$\leqslant \quad \{ \text{ Lemmas 2.1, 2.2, 2.3 ; definitions of } foldl \text{ and } \dot{\leqslant} \; \}$

$\quad foldl \; (+) \; (q \; x \; xs) \; (gmapQ \; (everything \; (+) \; (q' \; f \; x)) \; xs)$

$\leqslant \quad \{ \text{ Lemma 2.3; definitions of } foldl \text{ and } \dot{\leqslant} \; \}$

$\quad foldl \; (+) \; (q' \; f \; x \; xs) \; (gmapQ \; (everything \; (+) \; (q' \; f \; x)) \; xs)$

$= \quad \{ \text{ definition of } everything \; \}$

$\quad everything \; (+) \; (q' \; f \; x) \; xs$

$= \quad \{ \text{ definition of } q' \; \}$

$\quad everything \; (+) \; ((q \; (f \; x)) \circ (mkT \; f)) \; xs$

$= \quad \{ \text{ condition } (fusable \; (f)) \; \}$

$\quad everything \; (+) \; (q \; (f \; x)) \; (everywhere \; (mkT \; f) \; xs)$

$= \quad \{ \text{ definition of } occurs \; \}$

$\quad occurs \; (f \; x) \; (everywhere \; (mkT \; f) \; xs)$

2.6 A FUSION LAW FOR *everywhere*

In the previous sections we have used generic reasoning to prove theorems about generic functions. Here we use it to *calculate* the weakest condition needed for a statement to hold. The statement in question is a generalisation of Theorem 2.1 from a one-layer transformation to a full bottom-up transformation.

Statement. $\langle \forall t \; t' \; :: \; (everywhere \; t) \circ (everywhere \; t') = everywhere \; (t \circ t') \rangle$

As with other fusion laws, its practical importance is that it can be used to optimise programs. When this is done reliably and consistently, programmers are encouraged to write simple functions, and let the compiler turn them into efficient ones. (Like our *occursList* function in § 2.5.)

Alas, it is not the case that two arbitrary *everywhere* transformations can be fused. For instance, let t be a transformation that prepends a fixed character, say 'a', to a string and is the identity at other types. It can be defined as $t = mkT \; (\lambda s \rightarrow \text{'a'} : s)$. Then we have that *everywhere* $(t \circ t)$ applied to the empty string returns "aa", while $(everywhere \; t) \circ (everywhere \; t)$ returns "aaa".[4]

What happens here is that the first transformation creates new nodes where the second transformation is applicable – in our case, new substrings. That is, it

---

[4]The first application of $(everywhere \; t)$ returns 'a' : [ ]. If 'a' is prepended, bottom-up, to all nodes of type string in 'a' : [ ], we get "aaa".

changes the structure. A (too strong) condition for fusion is that the first traversal
does not change the structure. A weaker condition is that at any nodes that are
created or deleted, the second transformation is the identity. What we do in this
section is turn this informal description into a precise statement about t and t',
via formal calculation. In fact, it is possible that the informal condition is not the
weakest one – this is the problem with informal statements. However, the one we
calculate is guaranteed to be, by construction, the weakest condition. This is the
case because all steps in the proof are equality steps.

This calculation is more interesting than the proofs we have shown so far, in
the sense that straightforward induction on the structure of types is not enough to
complete the proof.

2.6.1   Calculating a condition for fusion

We proceed as if we were writing a proof, even though we know the statement is
not a theorem. Then, when a step cannot be justified, we make it a condition of
the statement. Our theorem can be stated as:

Theorem 2.5. $\langle \forall t\ t'\ ::\ (everywhere\ t) \circ (everywhere\ t') = everywhere\ (t \circ t') \Leftarrow$
$fusable\_ev\ (t, t')$

The predicate $fusable\_ev\ (t, t')$ is the conjunction of the conditions that arise during the calculation. We defer giving its definition until we complete the proof.
Conditions only arise in the cases for sums and products. The statement is already provable for the empty type and for basic types:

- **Case** $T = 0 \,/\, Unit \,/\, Int$

$$everywhere\langle T \rangle\ t\ (everywhere\langle T \rangle\ t'\ x)$$
$$=\ \{\ \text{definitions of } everywhere \text{ and } gmapT\langle 0 \,/\, Unit \,/\, Int \rangle\ \}$$
$$everywhere\langle T \rangle\ t\ (t'\ x)$$
$$=\ \{\ \text{definitions of } everywhere \text{ and } gmapT\langle 0 \,/\, Unit \,/\, Int \rangle\ \}$$
$$(t \circ t')\langle T \rangle\ x$$
$$=\ \{\ \text{definitions of } everywhere \text{ and } gmapT\langle 0 \,/\, Unit \,/\, Int \rangle\ \}$$
$$everywhere\langle T \rangle\ (t \circ t')\ x$$

The case for sums shows that straightforward induction is not sufficient to complete the proof. Assume that we used the following induction hypothesis:

$$I\langle T \rangle\ =\ \langle \forall t\ t'\ ::\ everywhere\langle T \rangle\ t \circ everywhere\langle T \rangle\ t' = everywhere\langle T \rangle\ (t \circ t')\rangle$$

In the third equality step, in order to proceed towards the goal, we would like to
use the fusion law (backwards) to split the traversal ($everywhere\ (t \circ t')$) into a
composition of two traversals ($everywhere\ t \circ everywhere\ t'$). But we may not invoke the induction hypothesis as a justification, since, there, it is $gmapT$ that takes

a type argument, and the induction hypothesis is about *everywhere*, not *gmapT*. The solution is to strengthen the induction hypothesis and construct a proof by mutual induction. Thus, the induction hypothesis is:

$$I'\langle T \rangle = \langle \forall t\, t' :: I\langle T \rangle \wedge$$
$$gmapT\langle T \rangle\, (everywhere\, t \circ everywhere\, t') = gmapT\langle T \rangle\, (everywhere\, (t \circ t')) \rangle$$

In the remainder of the proof we sometimes use *evW* instead of *everywhere* in order to limit the size of a line to the page width.

- **Case** $T = A + B, x = inl\, a$

$$everywhere\langle T \rangle\, (t \circ t')\, x$$
$$= \quad \{\text{ definition of } everywhere\, \}$$
$$(t \circ t')\langle T \rangle\, (gmapT\langle T \rangle\, (everywhere\, (t \circ t'))\, x)$$
$$= \quad \{\text{ definition of } gmapT\langle A + B \rangle\, \}$$
$$(t \circ t')\langle T \rangle\, (inl\, (gmapT\langle A \rangle\, (everywhere\, (t \circ t'))\, a))$$
$$= \quad \{\text{ (mutual) induction }\}$$
$$(t \circ t')\langle T \rangle\, (inl\, (gmapT\langle A \rangle\, (everywhere\, t \circ everywhere\, t')\, a))$$
$$= \quad \{\text{ definition of } gmapT\langle A + B \rangle\, \}$$
$$(t \circ t')\langle T \rangle\, (gmapT\langle T \rangle\, (everywhere\, t \circ everywhere\, t')\, x)$$
$$= \quad \{\, gmapT \text{ fusion }\}$$
$$(t \circ t')\langle T \rangle\, ((gmapT\langle T \rangle\, (evW\, t)) \circ (gmapT\langle T \rangle\, (evW\, t'))\, x)$$
$$= \quad \{\, \bullet \text{ condition }\}$$
$$t\langle T \rangle\, ((gmapT\langle T \rangle\, (evW\, t)) \circ t'\langle T \rangle\, \circ (gmapT\langle T \rangle\, (evW\, t'))\, x)$$
$$= \quad \{\text{ definition of } everywhere, \text{ twice }\}$$
$$everywhere\langle T \rangle\, t\, (everywhere\langle T \rangle\, t'\, x)$$

The case for $x = inr\, b$ is symmetric.

- **Case** $T = A_1 \times \cdots \times A_n, x = (x1, ..., xn)$

$$everywhere\langle T \rangle\, t\, (everywhere\langle T \rangle\, t'\, x)$$
$$= \quad \{\text{ definition of } everywhere\, \}$$
$$everywhere\langle T \rangle\, t\, (t'\langle T \rangle\, (gmapT\langle T \rangle\, (everywhere\, t')\, x))$$
$$= \quad \{\text{ definition of } everywhere\, \}$$
$$t\langle T \rangle\, (gmapT\langle T \rangle\, (everywhere\, t)\, (t'\langle T \rangle\, (gmapT\langle T \rangle\, (everywhere\, t')\, x)))$$
$$= \quad \{\, \bullet \text{ condition }\}$$
$$(t \circ t')\langle T \rangle\, ((gmapT\langle T \rangle\, (everywhere\, t) \circ gmapT\langle T \rangle\, (everywhere\, t'))\, x)$$
$$= \quad \{\, gmapT \text{ fusion }\}$$
$$(t \circ t')\langle T \rangle\, ((gmapT\langle T \rangle\, (everywhere\, t \circ everywhere\, t'))\, x)$$
$$= \quad \{\text{ definition of } gmapT\langle A_1 \times \cdots \times A_n \rangle\, \}$$

$$(t \circ t')\langle T \rangle ((evW \, t \circ evW \, t')\langle T_1 \rangle \, x_1, \, ..., \, (evW \, t \circ evW \, t')\langle T_n \rangle \, x_n)$$

$= \{ \text{ induction } \}$

$$(t \circ t')\langle T \rangle (everywhere\langle T_1 \rangle \, (t \circ t') \, x_1, \, ..., \, everywhere\langle T_n \rangle \, (t \circ t') \, x_n)$$

$= \{ \text{ definition of } gmapT\langle A_1 \times \cdots \times A_n \rangle \}$

$$(t \circ t')\langle T \rangle (gmapT\langle T \rangle \, (everywhere \, (t \circ t') \, x))$$

$= \{ \text{ definition of } everywhere \}$

$$everywhere\langle T \rangle \, (t \circ t') \, x$$

For both sums and products we get the same condition. It remains that we prove the second conjunct of the induction hypothesis. This part of the proof is in Appendix 2.11.

To summarise, we have replaced an informal condition on t and t' ('*everywhere t* preserves the shape, except possibly at nodes where t' is the identity'), by a precise predicate, defined in terms of *gmapT* and *everywhere*.

$$fusable\_ev \, (t,t') \, =$$
$$t \circ gmapT \, (everywhere \, t) \circ t' \circ gmapT \, (everywhere \, t') \, =$$
$$t \circ t' \circ gmapT \, (everywhere \, t) \circ gmapT \, (everywhere \, t')$$

This predicate, however, is rather complex, and it is not easy to check whether it holds in the context of specific datatypes and for specific transformations t and t'. In practise, it might be easier to check the following, stronger predicate.

$$fusable\_ev' \, (t,t') \, =$$
$$gmapT \, (everywhere \, t) \circ t' \, = \, t' \circ gmapT \, (everywhere \, t)$$

We still do not have experience in using these conditions in real-world situations. Only time will tell how effective they are in practise.

2.7 CONCLUSIONS AND FURTHER WORK

The essence of this paper is the idea that reasoning about (a restricted class of) overloaded functions can be practical, provided that those functions can be described in a generic programming style that supports adequate proof methods. When such a translation is not possible (because the function does not admit a generic definition), reasoning is not impossible, but instead of a single generic proof, proofs for many type instances must be provided [vvd05, Pau04].

We have looked at functions from the 'boilerplate' library, but the principle is general and is applicable to overloaded functions that can be generated mechanically (e.g. using Haskell's *deriving* clauses, or with tools like DrIFT[5]).

Our conviction that proofs are important for generic programs has been strengthened as a result of writing this paper. When we first set out to prove theorems 2.4 and 2.5, we believed that stronger versions of those theorems were true. After all,

---

[5]Available from http://repetae.net/john/computer/haskell/DrIFT

they looked like straightforward generalisations of known theorems about functions over lists. The confusion can arise because in many cases, *everywhere* computes the same result as a generic *map*. However, *everywhere* is a more general function than a generic *map* – for instance, its application can result in a change of the structure of a container – and satisfies fewer properties. The danger of this sort of mistake is that programmers might perform program transformations (perhaps to improve performance) that are not meaning-preserving.

An interesting area for further work is the application of reasoning to program transformation. A practical disadvantage of generic functions implemented with the 'boilerplate' combinators is the performance penalty caused by dynamic type checks. When enough is known about the types of arguments, it is sometimes possible to replace calls to generic functions by calls to specialised functions. For instance, assume that f has type $Int \rightarrow Int$. Then, it is easy to prove that *everywhere* $(mkT\ f)\ xs = map\ f\ xs$ if xs is a list of *Ints*. We also have that *everywhere* $(mkT\ f)\ ys = ys$ if ys is a list of characters, or in general, a value whose type does not contain *Ints*. These transformations eliminate the costs of dynamic type checks and could be performed automatically by a compiler. Being able to reason about generic functions is essential in order to justify the soundness of such transformations.

Acknowledgements. I would like to thank Roland Backhouse for very helpful discussions and feedback. Ralf Lämmel pointed out several errors and suggested improvements to a previous version of the paper. I would also like to thank the anonymous reviewers for their feedback. This work is fundend by EPSRC grant GR/S27078/01.

2.8 PROOF OF LEMMA 2.1

$$\langle \forall q\ q' :: q \stackrel{.}{\leqslant} q' \quad \Rightarrow \quad gmapQ\ q \ \stackrel{.}{\leqslant} \ gmapQ\ q' \rangle$$

By fixed-point induction on the structure of the type argument. The proof is included in the full version of the paper [Rei05].

2.9 PROOF OF LEMMA 2.2

$$\langle \forall q\ q' :: q \stackrel{.}{\leqslant} q' \quad \Rightarrow \quad everything\ (+)\ q \ \stackrel{.}{\leqslant} \ everything\ (+)\ q' \rangle$$

By fixed-point induction on the structure of the type argument. The proof is by mutual induction using the following induction hypothesis:

$$\langle \forall q\ q' :: q \stackrel{.}{\leqslant} q' \quad \Rightarrow \quad (everything\ (+)\ q \ \stackrel{.}{\leqslant} \ everything\ (+)\ q' \ \wedge$$
$$gmapQ\ (everything\ (+)\ q) \ \stackrel{.}{\leqslant} \ gmapQ\ (everything\ (+)\ q')) \rangle$$

2.10   PROOF OF LEMMA 2.3

$$\langle \forall x f :: q \, x \; \dot{\leqslant} \; q' f \, x \rangle$$

We prove the statement $\langle \forall x f \, xs :: q \, x \, xs \; \leqslant \; q' f \, x \, xs \rangle$. Lemma 2.3 follows from this statement and the definition of $\dot{\leqslant}$.

- **Case** x and xs have different type.

$q \, x \, xs$
$=$ { x, xs have different type; definition of q }
   0
$=$ { $(f \, x)$,$((mkT \, f) \, xs)$ have different type; definition of mkQ }
   $(0 \; `mkQ` \; (f \, x)) \, ((mkT \, f) \, xs)$
$=$ { definition of q' }
   $q' \, f \, x \, xs$

- **Case** x and xs have the same type.

We distinguish two cases. When $x \neq xs$, then x 'occurs' 0 times in xs.

$q \, x \, xs$
$=$ { $x \neq xs$; definition of q }
   0
$\leqslant$ { definition of q' }
   $q' \, f \, x \, xs$

If $x = xs$, then x 'occurs' once in xs, and both q and $q' \, f$ return 1.

$q \, x \, xs$
$=$ { $x = xs$; definition of q }
   1
$=$ { definition of q }
   $q \, (f \, x) \, (f \, x)$
$=$ { $(f \, x)$ well typed; definition of mkT }
   $q \, (f \, x) \, ((mkT \, f) \, x)$
$=$ { $x = xs$; definition of q' }
   $q' \, f \, x \, xs$

2.11   PROOF OF THEOREM 2.5 (CONTINUED)

Below is the proof, by fixed-point induction, of the second conjunct of the induction hypothesis:

$\langle \forall t\, t' \ :: \ everywhere\, t \circ everywhere\, t' = everywhere\, (t \circ t') \quad \wedge$
$\qquad gmapT\, (everywhere\, t \circ everywhere\, t') = gmapT\, (everywhere\, (t \circ t'))\rangle$

- **Case** $T = 0 \,/\, Unit \,/\, Int$

    $gmapT\langle T\rangle\, (everywhere\, (t \circ t'))\, x$
    $= \{ \text{ definition of } gmapT\langle 0 \,/\, Unit \,/\, Int\rangle \ \}$
    $\quad x$
    $= \{ \text{ definition of } gmapT\langle 0 \,/\, Unit \,/\, Int\rangle \ \}$
    $\quad gmapT\langle T\rangle\, (everywhere\, t \circ everywhere\, t')\, x$

- **Case** $T = A + B, x = inl\, a$

    $gmapT\langle T\rangle\, (everywhere\, (t \circ t'))\, x$
    $= \{ \text{ definition of } gmapT\langle A + B\rangle \ \}$
    $\quad inl\, (gmapT\langle A\rangle\, (everywhere\, (t \circ t'))\, a)$
    $= \{ \text{ induction } \}$
    $\quad inl\, (gmapT\langle A\rangle\, (everywhere\, t \circ everywhere\, t')\, a)$
    $= \{ \text{ definition of } gmapT\langle A + B\rangle \ \}$
    $\quad gmapT\langle T\rangle\, (everywhere\, t \circ everywhere\, t')\, x$

- **Case** $T = A + B, x = inr\, b$
Similar
- **Case** $T = A_1 \times \cdots \times A_n, x = (x1, ..., xn)$

    $gmapT\langle T\rangle\, (everywhere\, t \circ everywhere\, t')\, x$
    $= \{ \text{ definition of } gmapT\langle A_1 \times \cdots \times A_n\rangle \ \}$
    $\quad ((evW\, t \circ evW\, t')\langle T_1\rangle\, x_1,\ ...,\ (evW\, t \circ evW\, t')\langle T_n\rangle\, x_n)$
    $= \{ \text{ (mutual) induction } \}$
    $\quad (everywhere\langle T_1\rangle\, (t \circ t')\, x_1,\ ...,\ everywhere\langle T_n\rangle\, (t \circ t')\, x_n)$
    $= \{ \text{ definition of } gmapT\langle A_1 \times \cdots \times A_n\rangle \ \}$
    $\quad gmapT\langle T\rangle\, (everywhere\, (t \circ t'))\, x)$

REFERENCES

[AP01]   Artem Alimarine and Rinus Plasmeijer. A generic programming extension for Clean. In *Implementation of functional languages*, volume 2312 of *LNCS*, pages 168–185, 2001. Springer, Berlin.

[Hin00a] Ralf Hinze. Generic programs and proofs, 2000. Habilitationsschrift, Universität Bonn.

[Hin00b] Ralf Hinze. A new approach to generic functional programming. In *Conference Record of POPL'00: The 27th ACM SIGPLAN-SIGACT Symposium on Principles of Programming Languages*, pages 119–132, 2000. ACM Press, New York.

[Hin04]   Ralf Hinze. Generics for the masses. In *International Conference on Functional Programming (ICFP 2004)*, pages 236–243, 2004. ACM Press, New York.

[HJL05]   Stefan Holdermans, Johan Jeuring, and Andres Löh. Generic views on data types. In preparation, 2005.

[JJ96]   J. Jeuring and P. Jansson. Polytypic programming. In J. Launchbury, E. Meijer, and T. Sheard, editors, *Advanced Functional Programming, Second International School*, volume 1129 of *LNCS*, pages 68–114. Springer-Verlag, Berlin, 1996.

[Lö04]   Andres Löh. *Exploring Generic Haskell*. PhD thesis, University of Utrecht, 2004.

[LPJ03]   Ralf Lämmel and Simon Peyton Jones. Scrap your boilerplate: A practical design pattern for generic programming. In *ACM SIGPLAN Workshop on Types in Language Design and Implementation*, pages 26–37, 2003.

[LPJ04]   Ralf Lämmel and Simon Peyton Jones. Scrap more boilerplate: reflection, zips, and generalised casts. In *International Conference on Functional Programming (ICFP 2004)*, pages 244–255, 2004. ACM Press, New York.

[NJ04]   Ulf Norell and Patrik Jansson. Polytypic programming in haskell. In *Implementation of Functional Languages*, volume 3145 of *LNCS*, pages 168–184, 2004. Springer-Verlag, Berlin.

[Pau04]   Lawrence C. Paulson. Organizing numerical theories using axiomatic type classes. *Journal of Automated Reasoning*, 33(1):29–49, 2004.

[Rei05]   Fermín Reig. Generic proofs for combinator-based generic programs. Technical Report NOTTCS-TR-2005-2, School of Computer Science, University of Nottingham, 2005.

[Sch86]   David A. Schmidt. *Denotational Semantics - A Methodology for Language Development*. Allyn and Bacon, 1986.

[vvd05]   Ron van Kesteren, Marko van Eekelen, and Maarten de Mol. An effective proof rule for general type classes. In *Trends in Functional Programming*, volume 5. Intellect, Bristol, 2005.

Chapter 3

Building certified components within FOCAL

Catherine Dubois[1], Thérèse Hardin[2], Véronique Viguié Donzeau Gouge[3]

Abstract: Existing provers are good to prove program properties but bad in language support to write large programs. This combination is tackled in the program development environment FOCAL, a framework dedicated to the complete development of certified components, from the specification stage to the implementation one. FOCAL incorporates features such as inheritance, abstraction, late binding and redefinition. The paper gives an overview of the design of the environment and presents the language itself and the associated tools.

3.1 INTRODUCTION

Software developed for safety or security critical systems (aircrafts, automatic public transportation, nuclear plants, credit cards etc.) must pass a high level of scrutiny to ensure that it conforms to standards such as the IEC61508 standards for hard/soft systems, at all stages of development from requirements analysis through documentation and testing. For high levels of criticity, these standards require to use not only methods like safety analysis and careful code reviewing, but also formal methods along the complete software life-cycle process, in order to demonstrate correctness, safety, reliability, and security properties. There is a urgent need for tools able to help engineers along that process to decrease development and evaluation complexity and costs. Indeed static analysers, provers,

---

[1]CEDRIC, IIE, 18 allée Jean Rostand, 91025 Evry FRANCE;
E-mail: `dubois@iie.cnam.fr`

[2]CEDRIC, CNAM, 292 rue Saint Martin, 75003 Paris FRANCE;
E-mail: `donzeau@cnam.fr`

[3]LIP6, UPMC, 8 rue du Capitaine Scott, 75015 Paris FRANCE;
E-mail: `therese.hardin@lip6.fr`

verifiers are great help to deal with correctness but they are definitively not usable to write large programs. This problem is tackled here. And we claim that functional languages and, more generally an approach based on functionality, may lead to powerful development environments, able to handle most of the safety requirements.

Since 1998 we address the problem of highly critical software development, and we have started to built a new development environment, called FOCAL (previously called FOC) freely distributed at focal.inria.fr. Its language is a strict functional ML-like language, with declarations, definitions of functions, properties and proofs. It comes with a compiler which produces runnable code, automatic documentation facilities and two ways to prove properties automatically or not, the proofs being ultimately checked with the theorem prover Coq. Presently, it provides no help for treating concurrency, testing, model-checking, all points which have to be integrated to reach our objectives. Thus it is still in an early stage of development but we think that it already deserves to be presented, as it can help specification, design and implementation steps of critical components. Moreover, its functional style and its modularity provide help for ultimate code reviewing. We are currently integrating tools based on first-order rewriting and equational theories.

In the following, we first give the requirements of FOCAL and its fundamental design principles in the Section 3.2. We give an overview of the language itself in the Section 3.3. Then, Section 3.4 details a complete, but short, example. Section 3.5 presents the compiler, the proof tools and the documentation tools. Some applications developed within FOCAL are briefly presented in 3.6. A very short comparison with other approaches is given in Section 3.7. The conclusion presents some development perspectives.

3.2 FOCAL REQUIREMENTS AND DESIGN PRINCIPLES

The project of developing software meeting high level safety requirements started in 1998, after some unsuccessful attempts [Ale98, BHMMR99, SBR99] of proving properties of computer algebra programs. The main difficulties came from the ambiguities of the semantics of the language. We refused to choose between several possible interpretations of, for example, multiple inheritance and late binding, as we cannot have the guarantee that compilers conform to our choice. The FOCAL project arises from this conclusion with the objective of helping all stages of development of critical software within safety and security framework, at least when formal methods are required. In this section, we briefly expose the requirements for the development environment and relate them to the fundamental design principles of FOCAL.

From the beginning of our project, we have a double requirement: the development environment must provide high-level and justified confidence to users and it must be easy to use by well-trained engineers. Thus, some balance has to be found between the logical and semantic rigour and the cost of formal development, partly due to the lack of training of engineers on logics and provers.

First of all, we consider that a specification is defined by declarations and properties, and also by some comments in natural language which are true parts of the documentation. The design phase may introduce more declarations, some definitions of functions, data representation and related properties. At this stage functions represent effective relations between even not yet implemented entities. The implementation phase adds more definitions and properties until the implementation is *complete*, that is, all declarations have received definitions and all properties are proven. Actually, proofs can be done 'just in time', a point explained further.

So the user of the environment develops libraries of components, going step by step from specifications to programs actually reusing already designed or implemented components. This includes proving the required properties. Thus, the language has to provide declarations with deferred definitions and redefinitions, multiple inheritance, powerful parametrization, sharing/reusing of code etc. and definitively, a powerful type system. It also has to provide a user-friendly prover or at least a nice interaction with an existing prover.

The components of the library can also be used as Components Off The Shelf (COTS) in a kind of *read-eval-print* loop, having confidence in imported components. These end users do not want to do proofs but have to be protected from misuse of components. This last point asks for an abstraction mechanism over components.

To sum up, we want to address *certified development in the large* but also *certified development in the small*. So FOCAL proposes a language featuring mechanisms such as inheritance, late binding, redefinition, parametrization, encapsulation and declarations/definitions, properties/theorems. The confidence in proofs relies on proof verification.

3.3 OVERVIEW OF FOCAL

In this section we introduce the main features of the language in its current version. The way proofs can be done will be described in the Section 3.5. A complete example is given in the next section. A FOCAL development is organised as a hierarchy which may have several roots. The upper levels of the hierarchy are built along the specification stage while the lower ones correspond to implementations. Each node of the hierarchy corresponds to a progress to a complete implementation. We call *refinement* the process of building top-down a hierarchy.

Species A node of the hierarchy is called a *species*. A species is a kind of record composed of fields, called *methods*, which may be:

- The method introduced by the keyword rep which gives the data representation, that is a type called the *carrier type*. It can be a variable type or a more defined ML like type. This method is mandatory and can be explicitly given or obtained by inheritance.

- Declarations introduced by the keyword sig followed by a name and a type.

- Definitions introduced by the keyword let made of a name, a type and an expression. Mutually recursive definitions are introduced by let rec.

- Statements introduced by the keyword property followed by a name and a first-order statement (with the usual connectors e.g. not, and).

- Theorems introduced by the keyword theorem followed by a name, a statement and a proof ultimately checked with the theorem prover Coq.

Statements, definitions and proofs can freely use names of other methods of the species (denoted by self!m). However, in case of dependence cycle, the compiler rejects the species. A let rec definition is not considered as leading to a dependence cycle. Here, we differ a lot from the usual object-oriented languages where methods are considered as mutually recursive without any restriction (indeed a species is not a class, nor an object according to the usual meanings in the object oriented terminology). Method types are type expressions *à la* ML. The expression self in a type denotes the rep of the species and should be understood as self!rep.

The *elements* of the species are called *entities*, to emphasize on the fact that they are defined not only by their representation but also by the functions that manipulate them and their properties.

Inheritance   A species B refines a species A if the methods introduced in A and/or the carrier type of A are made more concrete (more defined) in B. In addition, new methods can be added in B and already given definitions can be redefined. This kind of refinement is just a multiple inheritance mechanism. If a species A inherits from several species S_i, our view of data representation implies that all S_i have unifiable rep and that the rep of A is by default the obtained unifier. However, the rep of A can be replaced by a less general unifier (thus more precise). If two S_i have a method having a same name, then their types must be given by the same expression and if they are both defined, we retain the last inherited definition (as in OCaml).

Interfaces   The type of a species is obtained by removing definitions and proofs. If self!rep is still a type variable say α, then the species type is prefixed with an existential binder $\exists \alpha$, which will be eliminated as soon as the rep will be instantiated. The species types remain implicit in the concrete syntax. However, we need here to introduce them to explain the notion of *interface*. The interface of a species is obtained by abstracting the rep type in all the method types of the species type. This abstraction remains implicit in the concrete syntax as the interface of a species is also denoted by the species name.

Interfaces can be ordered by inclusion, a point which gives a very simple notion of subtyping.

Collections   A species is said to be *complete* if all declarations have received definitions and all properties have received proofs. A complete species can be submitted to an abstraction process to create a *collection*. A collection is indeed

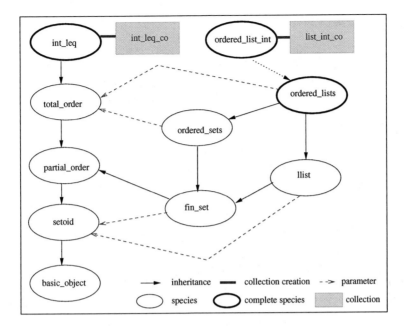

FIGURE 3.1.   The hierarchy of the example

a kind of abstract data type and users have only access to its interface, but having the guarantee that all methods are defined/proven.

Parametrized species   Species can be parametrized by collections. The formal parameter is introduced by a name c and an interface I. Any collection CC having an interface including I can be used as an actual parameter for c. In the species body, the methods and statements of the parameter are denoted by c!m. The fact that CC has been created upon a complete species ensures that no link error can arrive at runtime and that proofs of CC can be used as lemmas.
Species can also be parametrized by entities of collections, themselves introduced as parameters, thus introducing a dependence between parameters. The syntax forbids dependence cycles between parameters.

Method types   The type of a method is either a basic type like `bool` or a product type or a functional type or a user declared ML-like type. Moreover method types may contains expressions such as `self!rep` and `c!rep` (also written `c`). The former denotes an entity of the species, the latter denotes a value of the collection `c` and in this case its type is abstract (we do not know anything about the type used to represent it).

3.4 A COMPLETE EXAMPLE

This section illustrates the different concepts of the language and also the programming style with the very classical example of ordered lists. So the aim is to produce a certified tool for manipulating ordered lists that behaves as an abstract data type. In other words, we wish to build a *collection* of ordered lists. For that, we build a small hierarchy of species and collections drawn in the Figure 3.1. The plan of this section follows this picture bottom up and from left to right. For lack of place, we cannot explain and show all the development, so we give only fragments of species. However, the complete FOCAL code can be found at focal.inria.fr.

basic_object Let us first build from scratch a species called basic_object as the root of the hierarchy.

```
species basic_object =
rep;
sig parse : string -> self;
sig print : self -> string;
end
```

setoid Species can also be built by inheritance. For instance, let us write the species setoid that describes the notion of setoid, a set equipped with a binary relation equal which is reflexive, symmetric and transitive.

```
species setoid inherits basic_object =
sig equal in self->self->bool;

property equal_refl: all x in self, !equal(x,x)
property equal_sym: all x, y in self,
  !equal(x,y) -> !equal(y,x);
property equal_trans: all x, y, z in self,
  !equal(x,y) -> !equal(y,z) -> !equal(x,z);

let different(x,y)=#not_b(!equal(x,y));
theorem different_not_equal:
  all x, y in self, !different(x,y) <-> (not !equal(x,y))
  proof: def: different;
  {* Intros x y; Unfold abst_different setoid__different;
   Split; Elim (abst_equal x y); Compute; Assumption. *};
end
```

Thus the species setoid inherits the three methods of basic_object and introduces its own methods: the declared function equal and those properties stating that equal is an equivalence relation, the defined function different and a theorem different_not_equal. This last function is defined by using the boolean negation #not_b on FOCAL booleans[1] and the not yet defined function equal: late binding enters here.

Recall that self in an expression type denotes self!rep and the expression x in self in a formula denotes an entity of the species. The expression !equal is just an abbreviation for self!equal.

The species contains the proof of the theorem different_not_equal given as a Coq proof script (in italics). We do not go into details on the proof, we just emphasize that the names of the methods are qualified by abst (when the method is only declared) or by species names. This comes from the compilation scheme to Coq that we outline in 3.5.

Before giving the proof script, the programmer has to be precise about the dependencies of the theorem: there is a *def-dependence* of m upon m' if the former uses the type and the definition of the latter. On the other hand, when a method m only requires the type of another method m', we say that m *decl-depends* upon m'. In the present case, different_is_not_equal def-depends upon different: the tactic Unfold abst_different does unfold the definition of different. A question arises here: what about the proof of the theorem if a daughter species redefines the method different? Because of the def-dependence, the proof will not be valid anymore and it will have to be done again in the new context.

total_order Now we define the species partial_order that enriches the setoid notion with an order leq and we continue with the species total_order which constraints the order to be total. Furthermore, this last species defines the strict inequality lt from leq and also the inherited method equal from lt. It is time now to prove the properties of equal declared in setoid.

```
species partial_order inherits setoid
sig leq in self -> self -> bool;
property leq_refl: all x, y in self,
  !equal(x,y) -> !leq(x,y);
property leq_antisymmetric: all x, y in self,
  !leq(x,y) -> !leq(y,x) -> !equal(x,y) ;
property leq_trans: all x, y, z in self,
  !leq(x,y) -> !leq(y,z) -> !leq(x,z);
let lt(x,y) = #and_b(!leq(x,y),#not_b(!equal(x,y)));
end

species total_order inherits partial_order
property leq_total: all x, y in self, !leq(x,y) or !leq(y,x);
let equal(x,y) = #and_b(self!leq(x,y),self!leq(y,x));
proof of equal_sym =
  def: equal;  ...
...
end
```

---

[1] functions prefixed by # are predefined functions coming from the FOCAL prelude. Do not confuse #not_b with the unary logical connector written not.

int_leq To continue the example, we can now define the species int_leq as a setoid with the usual total order ⩽ by inheritance of total_order. The rep is refined as the FOCAL type int, defined in the FOCAL prelude as a type to be compiled on the OCaml type int and the Coq type z:

```
species int_leq inherits total_order =
rep = int;
let leq = #int_leq;
let print = #string_of_int;
let parse = #int_of_string;
proof of leq_reflexive = assumed;
proof of leq_total = assumed;
...
end
```

In this species, leq is defined as the OCaml function leq with the usual order of int (this is the meaning of #int_leq). At this point, we do not make a correspondence with the Coq leq defined on z. Thus, we have to prove that the OCaml function leq is indeed a total order. Here we have two possibilities. Either we try to do the proofs and we have to embark on studying machine integer implementation, a point which is very far from our initial problem. Or we consider that integer machine implementation is trusted and we do the proofs by just answering assumed. That means that the statement will be considered by Coq as an axiom. Doing a proof by assumed is a pragmatical choice based on the application domain and in the confidence we can have on some properties (according to the context, do we need to formally prove some Pythagorean theorem?) and also on the balance between trust and costs. Here testing the property by evaluating it with some pertinent test cases could strengthen our confidence in the property.

int_leq_co Returning to the species int_leq, we can consider it as complete: methods are all defined/proved. Thus we are allowed (by the compiler) to build from it a *collection* which encapsulates the rep type and provides the functions defined in the species int_leq. A collection is indeed a certified abstract data type, its interface being the one of the complete species from which it has been built.

```
collection int_leq_co implements int_leq;
```

fin_set At this stage, we want to introduce the notion of finite set. First we introduce the species fin_set parametrized by a collection a satisfying the interface setoid: a must provide all the operations parse, print, equal which handle values of an abstract data type denoted in the body of the species by a. The species declares the set primitives operations. Each of them is completed by its specification (e.g. singleton and singleton_spec). The species inherits from partial_order: leq is defined as the subset predicate and is proved a partial order.

```
species fin_set (a is setoid) inherits partial_order =
sig empty in self;
sig singleton in a -> self;
sig isin in a -> self -> bool;
sig cardinal in self -> int;
sig subset in self -> self -> bool;
...
let leq = !subset;

property singleton_spec: all x, y in a,
  !est_element(y,!singleton(x)) <-> a!equal(x,y);
...
```

ordered_set We now build the species ordered_set that specifies the finite sets the elements of which are taken in a totally ordered set: it declares a new method min that returns the minimal element of a non empty set.

```
species ordered_set(a is total_order) inherits fin_set(a) =
sig min in self -> a;
property min_spec : all e in self,
  not(!empty(e))->(!isin(!min(e),e) and
  (all x in a, !isin(x,e) -> a!leq(!min(e),x)));
end
```

llist We write the complete species llist of finite lists. A finite list is considered as a finite set, so this new species inherits from fin_set(a). We choose to represent our lists as lists *à la* ML constrained to contain distinct elements. The rep type is then list(a) that is the type constructor list (the same as in OCaml) applied to the rep of the collection a, named also a. Some of the primitives declared in llist(a), e.g. empty, singleton are defined as operations upon lists while union, diff and inter are kept as signatures. The defined primitives are proved correct with respect to their specifications. Furthermore, they are proved correct with respect to the *representation invariant*, that is the property well_formed establishing that the representation of a set is a *well-formed* list containing distinct elements. For instance we prove that !empty is well-formed and subset preserves the well-formedness etc. Up to now, these properties are written manually, we plan to generate them automatically from the representation invariant.

```
species llist(a is setoid) inherits fin_set(a)=
rep = list(a);
(* representation invariant *)
let rec wf (l in self) =
   match l with
     [] -> #True
   | a::l -> #and_b (#not_b(!isin(a,l)),!wf(l))
   end;
```

```
let empty in self = [];
let singleton(x)= [x];
let isin(x,e) =
   match e with
     [] -> #False
   | y::l -> if a!equal(x,y) then #True else !isin(x,l)
   end;
proof of singleton_spec =  ...
theorem wellformed_empty: !wf(!empty)
  proof: ...
...
end
```

If we derive from llist a species implementing and proving correct the operations inter, union and diff, this derived species once instantiated would be a candidate to build a collection, e.g. the collection of lists of integers.

ordered_list   To achieve our initial objective, it remains to write the species ordered_list parametrized by a collection of interface total_order: it implements the ordered lists and the associated operations, in particular the union function as the merge of two ordered lists. This species uses multiple inheritance: ordered_list(a) inherits ordered_set(a) and llist(a). So the rep is inherited from llist(a) and is list(a). The min function inherited from ordered_set(a) is defined as the function returning the head of the list.

The representation invariant is updated: we add the fact that the elements are ordered according to the total order of a. So we have to prove that each operation is correct with respect to this new property. The first invariant (wf) is still appropriate, so we have to state that inter, union and diff preserve this property. The proof part of this species is important but also heavy.

```
species ordered_list (a is total_order)
inherits ordered_set(a), llist(a) =
(* representation invariant *)
let rec ordered(l in self) in bool =
   match l with
     [] -> #True
   | [x] ->  #True
   | x::y::l -> #and_b(a!lt(x,y), !ordered(l))
   end;
theorem ordered_empty : !ordered(!empty)
   ...
theorem wellformed_union : all s, t in self,
   !wf(s) -> !wf(t) -> !wf(!union(s,t))
   ...
theorem ordered_union : all s, t in self,
   !ordered(s) -> !ordered(t) -> !ordered(!union(s,t))
   ...
end
```

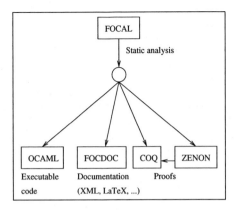

FIGURE 3.2.   The system FOCAL

ordered_list_int   To end with the hierarchy built in this section, it remains for example to instantiate this species with the previous collection int_leq and then to produce the corresponding collection.

```
species ordered_list_int inherits ordered_list(int_leq)=
end
collection ordered_list_int_co implements ordered_list_int;
```

3.5   COMPILING

The FOCAL development environment comes with a compiler which starts with a sequence of static analyses and then produces different outputs [Pre03]. The Figure 3.2 illustrates the different tools that the environment includes.

Analysis   After a syntactic analysis, the compiler first performs a typing analysis of methods, with a very simple Damas-Milner like algorithm. Then, it constructs a dependence graph between all methods, inherited or native to try to order consistently the methods. In case of a dependence cycle, the compiler fails. It checks if some methods are redefined and removes all proofs having def-dependencies on these methods. It also checks that the species used to build a collection is indeed complete. And, it verifies that actual parameters have an interface fitting with the interface of the formal parameter. When the species is recognized as correct, it enters the translation phase, mostly based on the dependence graph. The different possible translations are independent.

Running   The compiler produces a source code for OCaml using classes, objects and modules. The obtained object code is very efficient [BHR01] (time and memory) thanks to the OCaml implementation.

Proving   The compiler produces Coq code corresponding to the FOCAL components, that is processed by Coq in order to check the proofs. The Coq translation scheme relies on the following features :

- A species is translated into a record whose fields are all the methods of the species, inherited, declared and defined.

- A method m defined in a species s is translated into a *method generator gen_m* that is a Coq function/property parametrized by the methods upon which m depends.

- And in the species which inherits m, the corresponding field is built by application of *gen_m*.

So in the Coq translation, inheritance is *flatten* and dependencies are made explicit. For further explanations the reader can consult [PD02, PDH02, Pre03]. Typechecking with Coq ensures that the proofs are valid but also that design stages are coherent and that all methods are well-typed.

There are two ways to do the proofs. Either, they are done with the Coq tactics as is exemplified in 3.4. Or the programmer may discharge them with the help of Zenon, a very recent dedicated prover [Dol04]. Zenon is a first order theorem prover, developed by Doligez, based on the tableau method incorporating implementation novelties such as sharing. Inspired by the Lamport's hierarchical style it is declarative so it means that the user gives intermediate lemmas as hints and Zenon combines them to search the proof. Furthermore Zenon can do proof reconstruction: once the proof is found, it can be output in a Coq-checkable format to be typechecked by Coq.

As already mentioned in Section 3.4, the redefinition of a function by inheritance may invalidate the proofs that involve this function. The proofs are then erased and must be done again in the new context. Thus the main difficulty is to choose the best node in the hierarchy to do a proof. The naive view which consists in proving the properties as soon as possible is not always the right methodology: the proofs are done at an abstract level and the method may not be used in the implementations. The alternative solution that is to prove everything when completing a species is definitely not the right solution either: there are too much implementation details that complicate the proofs and the user may be led to duplicate the proofs. In [PJ03], Prevosto and Jaume propose a *coding style* to minimize the number of proofs to be redone in the case of a redefinition: e.g. minimize number of theorems with def-dependencies, minimize complexity of theorems with def-dependencies and do not have more than one def-dependence per theorem. The tools of the FOCAL environment to visualize the dependencies may help in such a context.

Documenting   The tool called FOCDOC [MP03] automatically generates XML documentation, thus the documentation of a component is always coherent with respect to its implementation. This tool uses its own XML format that contains information coming not only from structured comments and FOCAL concrete syntax but also from type inference and dependence analysis. From this XML representation, FOCDOC generates HTML files or Latex files.

3.6 APPLICATIONS

Computer algebra   FOCAL has been first used to develop a library for computer algebra, a subject which indeed does not exemplify critical systems. But it has the advantage that its formal specification can be found in mathematical books and that its algorithms may be very intricate, use complex data structures and are heavy time and memory consuming. So, this is a very good running example. The library offers powerful tools to manipulate multivariate polynomials. The specification stage introduces all needed mathematical notions, the design stage introduces some data representations and algorithms and the implementation offers different implementations of polynomials according to the chosen representation of degrees and coefficients (machine integers, arbitrary precision integers or rationals, for example). Classical benchmarks on polynomials (such as to compute a sub-resultant -a kind of gcd- of $P = x^{30} + ax^{20} + 2ax^{10} + 3a$ and $Q = x^{25} + 4bx^{15} + 5bx^5$ where a is a natural between 10^{100} and 10^{700} and $b = a + 1$) have shown very good efficiency of the runnable code [BHR01].

The automatic documentation viewer gives a precise description of the underlying mathematical structures and the implementation choices. Furthermore FOCAL also proposes dedicated tools to translate OMDoc documents (Open Maths Document, a standard format for encoding mathematical content) into FOCAL species or collections and vice versa.

Security policies   Currently, we use FOCAL to build a library for expressing and coding security policies [JM05]. The specification stage introduces subjects, objects and access rights. Then frameworks are built upon finite subsets of subjects, objects and access rights, adding a lattice of security levels. Models are built upon frameworks by adding some evolution rules of access rights. A security system supervising the application of security rules is just an implementation of a model, by a kind of state machine, essentially defined by its transition function. We have used this library to implement a supervisor for SQL requests control in a relational database, using the well-known Bell-Lapadula system as a security policy.

Airport Security   The security of civil aviation is governed by international standards and recommended practices that detail the responsibilities of the different actors such as states, operators and security agents. These security rules are described in natural language documents from a few dozen to several hundred pages. These documents give the specifications of various procedures and artifacts which implement security in airports, aircrafts and air traffic control. It is essential to ensure the consistency and completeness of these specifications. The project Edemoi [Ede05] aims at constructing and analyzing a precise reference document that models and structures the current international standards and recommended practices about airport security. A first step consisted in reading the documents, especially the Annex 17 [Ann02] and modelling it with a graphical UML based formalism. This first model is a basis for discussion and validation with the certification authority, namely here the International Civil Aviation Organisation (ICAO). The second step of the Edemoi approach is to provide formal models and use specialized tools to study their consistency. The chosen languages for this stage are Z, B and FOCAL. The FOCAL modelling of the annex 17 is in progress and emphasizes again the great flexibility brought by the possibility to intermingle specifications and code. Indeed in this model some properties are very abstract while some others are security procedures.

3.7 RELATED WORK

FOCAL proposes a rather original way of using object-oriented features, modularity and dependent types. There are a lot of proposals and languages which combine more or less these three features, for instance modules, mixins, classes, EML (extended ML). Except in Coq [Chr03], modules do not mix code, specifications and proofs. Several languages propose functors to use modules as parameters of other modules. They can mimic some kind of inheritance, but it is quite poor and we lose readability. Mixins add some object-oriented features but, as far as we know, do not accept true redefinition of functions. EML [KST97] is a language developed some years ago to specify and develop modular SML programs. Thus Focal can be considered very close to EML but goes further by providing the proof framework. As far as we know, this aspect is not achieved in EML although some work exists about the termination of functions (a proof obligation generator for PVS).

With FOCAL, the verification of the properties can be done at different steps in the development process, even delayed until the end of the development making FOCAL a code verifier. A complete species is a kind of object-oriented program where the methods are annotated with properties, resembling Java programs annotated with JML. Such species also contain proofs. Some tools, e.g. Krakatoa [MPMU04], provide static verification of JML assertions, with different levels of expressiveness and automation. Krakatoa allows to prove that a JML-annotated method of a Java program meets its specifications given as a JML interface. This amounts to proving that class invariants, as well as post-conditions, hold at the end of a method execution, provided that invariants and pre-conditions were valid at the beginning. But these tools are external tools.

The Atelier B [AtB05] is a complete development environment allowing one to go from specification to code by proved correct refinement steps. This environment and more generally the B method [Abr96], and FOCAL are tools to realise formal conception. Furthermore, both enable to combine components. But the FOCAL object-oriented features together with the abstraction mechanisms (parameters and collections) give it an expressiveness and a flexibility that the importation rules of B do not provide.

3.8 CONCLUSION AND FUTURE WORK

FOCAL is a framework and a set of tools for developing executable and certified code. It is also a language to be used from the specification stage to the implementation one. Confidence is achieved by different means: the OCaml generated code is verified by typing tools; dependencies are also verified by Coq; each declared property in a collection is proved or assumed (hypothesis explicitly appearing in the documentation); proof terms are produced and ultimately verified by Coq; documentation is automatically produced, and thus always complete and coherent with respect to the development. Moreover the specification of the language itself has been done in Coq and the correctness of the compiler against this specification is proved (by hand) in [PB05].

Future work focus on two principal directions: proof search and specification style. Proving is very often fastidious and painful. So it is necessary, even fundamental, to provide some kind of automation. Our first axis consists in integrating rewriting tools and deduction modulo features into FOCAL. This work is done in the context of the project Modulogic [Mod05].

The second concern, specification style, is undertaken from different points: experimenting with FOCAL in other application domains, such as in the Edemoi project, adding the notion of state and taking into account behavioural properties. Indeed the core language of FOCAL is purely functional: the species have no state; no imperative feature is allowed. This language design choice was entailed by the need of confidence and to ease proofs. However in some applications for a matter of efficiency or readability, the notions of time and state are mandatory: methods become operations that may access or update the state according to an invariant property for example. A possible approach could be to incorporate some state-oriented constructs in the FOCAL language while still relying on a general functional framework (by computing effects for example).

FOCAL does not take into account neither time nor any temporal property. This is the subject of the complementary project Alidecs that started very recently with a synchronous approach [Ali05].

Acknowledgements. The authors wish to thank all the FOCAL team (from labs. CEDRIC, LIP6 and INRIA) for helpful discussions in particular about the central example of this paper. We are grateful to the anonymous reviewers for their constructive remarks.

REFERENCES

[Abr96]   J.R. Abrial. *The B-Book: Assigning Programs to Meanings.* Cambridge University Press, 1996.

[Ale98]   G. Alexandre. *D'Axiom à Zermelo.* Phd thesis, Université Paris 6, 1998.

[Ali05]   Alidecs. *ACI Sécurité & Informatique project.* www-verimag.imag.fr-/SYNCHRONE/alidecs. Accessed 27 April 2005.

[Ann02]   Annex 17 to the Convention on International Civil Aviation - Security - Safeguarding International Civil Aviation againts acts of unlawful interference, 2002.

[AtB05]   Atelier B. www.atelierb.societe.com. Accessed 27 April 2005.

[BHMMR99] S. Boulmé, T. Hardin, V. Ménissier-Morain, and R. Rioboo. On the way to certify computer algebra systems. In *Calculemus 99: Systems for Integrated Computation and Deduction*, vol 23, Trento, Italy, 1999. Elsevier.

[BHR01]   S. Boulmé, T. Hardin, and R. Rioboo. Some hints for polynomials in the Foc project. In S. Linton and R. Sebastiani, editors, *Proceedings of the Ninth Symposium on the Integration of Symbolic Computation and Mechanized Reasoning (Calculemus 01)*, Siena, Italy, June 2001.

[Chr03]   J. Chrzaszcz. Implementing modules in the coq system. In D. A. Basin and B. Wolff, editors, *Theorem Proving in Higher Order Logics, 16th International Conference, TPHOLs 2003, Rome, Italy*, volume 2758, pages 270–286. LNCS, Springer, Berlin, 2003.

[Dol04]   D. Doligez. Zenon, a first-order prover with coq-checkable output. In *2nd Workshop on Coq and Rewriting*, 2004.

[Ede05]   Edemoi.   *ACI   Sécurité   &   Informatique   project.* www-lsr.imag.fr/EDEMOI. Accessed 27 April 2005.

[JM05]   M. Jaume and C. Morisset. Formalisation and implementation of access control models. In *Information Assurance Security, International Conference on Information Technology, Coding and Computing (IAS ITCC 2005)*, pages 703–708, Las Vegas, NV, 2005. IEEE Computer Society.

[KST97]   S. Kahrs, D. Sannella, and A. Tarlecki. The definition of Extended ML: A gentle introduction. *Theoretical Computer Science*, 173:445–484, 1997.

[Mod05]   Modulogic.   *ACI   Sécurité   &   Informatique   project.* modulogic.inria.fr. Accessed 27 April 2005.

[MP03]   M. Maarek and V. Prevosto. Focdoc: the documentation system of foc. In *Proceedings of Calculemus*, Rome, Italy, September 2003.

[MPMU04]   C. Marché, C. Paulin-Mohring, and X. Urbain. The KRAKATOA tool for certification of JAVA/JAVACARD programs annotated in JML. *Journal of Logic and Algebraic Programming*, 58(1–2):89–106, 2004.

[PB05]   V. Prevosto and S. Boulmé. Proof contexts with late binding. In P. Urzyczyn, editor, *Typed Lambda Calculi and Applications*, volume 3461 of *LNCS*, pages 324–338. Springer, Berlin, April 2005.

[PD02]   V. Prevosto and D. Doligez. Algorithms and proof inheritance in the foc language. *Journal of Automated Reasoning*, 29(3-4):337–363, dec 2002.

[PDH02]   V. Prevosto, D. Doligez, and Th. Hardin. Algebraic structures and dependent records. In S. Tahar C. Munoz and V. Carreno, editors, *Theorem Proving in Higher Order Logics, 15th International Conference, TPHOLs 2002*, volume 2410, pages 298–313. LNCS, Springer, Berlin, August 2002.

[PJ03]   V. Prevosto and M. Jaume. Making proofs in a hierarchy of mathematical structures. In *11th Symposium on the Integration of Symbolic Computation and Mechanized Reasoning (Calculemus 2003)*, Rome, Italy, Sep 2003.

[Pre03]   V. Prevosto. *Conception et Implantation du langage FoC pour le développement de logiciels certifiés*. Phd thesis, Université Paris 6, 2003.

[SBR99]   T. Hardin S. Boulmé and R. Rioboo. Modules, Objets et Calcul Formel. In *10ème Journées Francophones des Langages Applicatifs, JFLA'99*, 1999.

Chapter 4

Calculating an Exceptional Machine

Graham Hutton, Joel Wright[1]

Abstract: In previous work we showed how to verify a compiler for a small language with exceptions. In this article we show how to *calculate*, as opposed to verify, an abstract machine for this language. The key step is the use of Reynold's *defunctionalization*, an old program transformation technique that has recently been rejuvenated by the work of Danvy et al.

4.1 INTRODUCTION

Exceptions are an important feature of modern programming languages, but their compilation has traditionally been viewed as an advanced topic. In previous work we showed how the basic method of compiling exceptions using *stack unwinding* can be explained and verified using elementary functional programming techniques [HW04]. In particular, we developed a compiler for a small language with exceptions, together with a proof of its correctness.

In the formal reasoning community, however, one prefers *constructions* to verifications [Bac03]. That is, rather than first writing the compiler and then separately proving its correctness with respect to a semantics for the language, it would be preferable to try and calculate the compiler [Mei92] directly from the semantics, with the aim of giving a systematic *discovery* of the idea of compiling exceptions using stack unwinding, as opposed to a post-hoc verification.

In this article we take a step towards this goal, by showing how to calculate an abstract machine for evaluating expressions in our language with exceptions. The key step in the calculation is the use of *defunctionalization*, a program transformation technique that eliminates the use of higher-order functions, first introduced by Reynolds in his seminal work on definitional interpreters [Rey72].

---

[1] School of Computer Science and IT, University of Nottingham, Jubilee Campus, Wollaton Road, Nottingham NG8 1BB, UK; E-mail: {gmh,jjw}@cs.nott.ac.uk.

Despite being simple and powerful, defunctionalization seems to be somewhat neglected in recent years. For example, it features in few modern courses, text-books, and research articles on program transformation, and does not seem to be as widely known and used as it should be. Recently, however, defunctionalization has been rejuvenated by the work of Danvy et al., who show how it can be applied in a variety of different areas, including the systematic design of abstract machines for functional languages [DN01, ABDM03b, ADM04].

In this article, we show how Danvy's approach can be used to calculate an abstract machine for our language with exceptions. Moreover, the calculation is *rabbit free*, in the sense that there are no Eureka steps in which one needs to metaphorically pull a rabbit out of a hat — all the required concepts arise naturally from the calculation process itself. The approach is based upon the work of Danvy et al., but the emphasis on calculation and the style of exposition are our own.

The language that we use comprises just integer values, an addition operator, a single exceptional value called throw, and a catch operator for this value [HW04]. This language does not provide features that are necessary for actual program-ming, but it *does* provide just what we need for expository purposes. In particular, integers and addition constitute a minimal language in which to consider compu-tation using a stack, and throw and catch constitute a minimal extension in which such computations can involve exceptions.

Our development proceeds in two steps, starting with the exception-free part of the language to introduce the basic techniques, to which support for exceptions is then added in the second step. All the programs are written in Haskell [Pey03], and all the calculations are presented using equational reasoning. An extended version of the article that includes the calculations omitted here for reasons of space is available from www.cs.nott.ac.uk/~gmh/machine-extended.pdf.

4.2 ABSTRACT MACHINES

An *abstract machine* can be defined as a term rewriting system for executing programs in a particular language, and is given by a set of rewrite rules that make explicit how each step of execution proceeds. Perhaps the best known example is Landin's SECD machine for the lambda calculus [Lan64], which comprises a set of rewrite rules that operate on tuples with four components that give the machine its name, called the stack, environment, control and dump.

For a simpler example, consider a language in which programs comprise a sequence of push and add operations on a stack of integers. In Haskell, such programs, operations and stacks can be represented by the following types:

$$
\begin{array}{lcl}
\textbf{type } Prog & = & [Op] \\
\textbf{data } Op & = & PUSH\ Int \mid ADD \\
\textbf{type } Stack & = & [Int]
\end{array}
$$

An abstract machine for this language is given by defining two rewrite rules on pairs of programs and stacks from the set $Prog \times Stack$:

$$\langle\, PUSH\ n\ :\ ops\ ,\ s\,\rangle \quad \longrightarrow \quad \langle\, ops\ ,\ n:s\,\rangle$$
$$\langle\, ADD:ops\ ,\ n:m:s\,\rangle \quad \longrightarrow \quad \langle\, ops\ ,\ n+m\ :\ s\,\rangle$$

The first rule states that push places a new integer on top of the stack, while the second states that add replaces the top two integers on the stack by their sum. This machine can be implemented in Haskell by an execution function that repeatedly applies the two rules until this is no longer possible:

$$
\begin{array}{lll}
exec & :: & (Prog, Stack) \to (Prog, Stack) \\
exec\ (PUSH\ n:ops,s) & = & exec\ (ops,n:s) \\
exec\ (ADD:ops,n:m:s) & = & exec\ (ops,n+m:s) \\
exec\ (p,s) & = & (p,s)
\end{array}
$$

For example, *exec* ([*PUSH* 1,*PUSH* 2,*ADD*], []) gives the result ([], [3]). In the remainder of this article, we will use the term abstract machine for such a functional implementation of an underlying set of rewrite rules.

4.3   ARITHMETIC EXPRESSIONS

As in our previous work [HW04], let us begin our development by considering a simple language of expressions comprising integers and addition, whose semantics is given by a function that evaluates an expression to its integer value:

$$
\begin{array}{lll}
\textbf{data}\ Expr & = & Val\ Int\ |\ Add\ Expr\ Expr \\
eval & :: & Expr \to Int \\
eval\ (Val\ n) & = & n \\
eval\ (Add\ x\ y) & = & eval\ x + eval\ y
\end{array}
$$

We will now calculate an abstract machine for this language, by making a series of three transformations to the semantics.

Step 1: Add continuations

At present, the order in which addition evaluates its argument expressions is determined by the language in which the semantics is written, in this case Haskell. The first step in producing an abstract machine is to make the order of evaluation explicit in the semantics itself. A standard technique for achieving this aim is to rewrite the semantics in *continuation-passing* style [Rey72].

A *continuation* is a function that will be applied to the result of an evaluation. For example, in the equation *eval* (*Add x y*) = *eval x* + *eval y* from our semantics, when the first recursive call, *eval x*, is being evaluated, the remainder of the right-hand side, + *eval y*, can be viewed as a continuation for this evaluation, in the sense that it is the function that will be applied to the result.

More formally, in the context of our semantics *eval* :: *Expr* → *Int*, a continuation is a function of type *Int* → *Int* that will be applied to the result of type *Int* to give a new result of type *Int*. (This type can be generalised to *Int* → *a*, but we do not need the extra generality for our purposes here.) We capture the notion of such a continuation using the following type definition:

$$\textbf{type } Cont \quad = \quad Int \rightarrow Int$$

Our aim now is to define a new semantics, $eval'$, that takes an expression and returns an integer as previously, but also takes a continuation that will be applied to the resulting integer. That is, we seek to define a function

$$eval' \quad :: \quad Expr \rightarrow Cont \rightarrow Int$$

such that:

$$eval'\ e\ c \quad = \quad c\ (eval\ e)$$

At this point in most texts, a recursive definition for $eval'$ would normally be written and then either proved to satisfy the above equation, or this be justified by appealing to the correctness of a general continuation-passing transformation. However, we prefer to *calculate* the definition for $eval'$ directly from the above equation, by the use of structural induction on *Expr*.

Case: *Val n*

$$
\begin{aligned}
&eval'\ (Val\ n)\ c \\
=\quad &\{ \text{ specification of } eval' \} \\
&c\ (eval\ (Val\ n)) \\
=\quad &\{ \text{ definition of } eval \} \\
&c\ n
\end{aligned}
$$

Case: *Add x y*

$$
\begin{aligned}
&eval'\ (Add\ x\ y)\ c \\
=\quad &\{ \text{ specification of } eval' \} \\
&c\ (eval\ (Add\ x\ y)) \\
=\quad &\{ \text{ definition of } eval \} \\
&c\ (eval\ x + eval\ y) \\
=\quad &\{ \text{ abstraction over } eval\ x \} \\
&(\lambda n \rightarrow c\ (n + eval\ y))\ (eval\ x) \\
=\quad &\{ \text{ induction hypothesis for } x \} \\
&eval'\ x\ (\lambda n \rightarrow c\ (n + eval\ y)) \\
=\quad &\{ \text{ abstraction over } eval\ y \} \\
&eval'\ x\ (\lambda n \rightarrow (\lambda m \rightarrow c\ (n + m))\ (eval\ y)) \\
=\quad &\{ \text{ induction hypothesis for } y \} \\
&eval'\ x\ (\lambda n \rightarrow eval'\ y\ (\lambda m \rightarrow c\ (n + m)))
\end{aligned}
$$

In conclusion, we have calculated the following recursive definition:

$$
\begin{aligned}
eval' \quad &:: \quad Expr \rightarrow Cont \rightarrow Int \\
eval'\ (Val\ n)\ c \quad &= \quad c\ n \\
eval'\ (Add\ x\ y)\ c \quad &= \quad eval'\ x\ (\lambda n \rightarrow eval'\ y\ (\lambda m \rightarrow c\ (n + m)))
\end{aligned}
$$

That is, for an integer value we simply apply the continuation, while for an addition we evaluate the first argument and call the result n, then evaluate the second argument and call the result m, and finally apply the continuation to the sum of n and m. In this manner, order of evaluation is now explicit in the semantics.

Note that we have ensured that addition evaluates its arguments from left-to-right by first abstracting over *eval x* in the above calculation, and then abstracting over *eval y*. It would be perfectly valid to proceed in the other direction, which would result in right-to-left evaluation. Note also that our original semantics can be recovered from our new semantics, by substituting the identity continuation $\lambda n \to n$ into the equation from which *eval'* was constructed. That is, our original semantics *eval* can now be redefined as follows:

$$
\begin{aligned}
eval & \quad :: \quad Expr \to Int \\
eval\ e & \quad = \quad eval'\ e\ (\lambda n \to n)
\end{aligned}
$$

Step 2: Defunctionalize

We have now taken a step towards an abstract machine by making evaluation order explicit, but in so doing have also taken a step away from such a machine by making the semantics into a higher-order function. The next step is to regain the first-order nature of the original semantics by eliminating the use of continuations, but retaining the explicit order of evaluation that they introduced.

A standard technique for eliminating the use of functions as arguments is *defunctionalization* [Rey72]. This technique is based upon the observation that we do not usually need the entire function-space of possible argument functions, because only a few forms of such functions are actually used in practice. Hence, we can represent the argument functions that we actually need using a datatype, rather than using the actual functions themselves.

In our new semantics, there are only three forms of continuations that are actually used, namely one to invoke the semantics, and two in the case for evaluating an addition. We begin by separating out these three forms, by giving them names and abstracting over their free variables. That is, we define three combinators for constructing the required forms of continuations:

$$
\begin{aligned}
c1 & \quad :: \quad Cont \\
c1 & \quad = \quad \lambda n \to n \\
c2 & \quad :: \quad Expr \to Cont \to Cont \\
c2\ y\ c & \quad = \quad \lambda n \to eval'\ y\ (c3\ n\ c) \\
c3 & \quad :: \quad Int \to Cont \to Cont \\
c3\ n\ c & \quad = \quad \lambda m \to c\ (n+m)
\end{aligned}
$$

At present we have just used anonymous names $c1$, $c2$ and $c3$ for the combinators, but these will be replaced by more suggestive names later on. Using these combinators, our semantics can now be rewritten as follows:

$$
\begin{array}{lll}
eval' & :: & Expr \rightarrow Cont \rightarrow Int \\
eval' \ (Val\ n)\ c & = & c\ n \\
eval' \ (Add\ x\ y)\ c & = & eval'\ x\ (c2\ y\ c) \\
\\
eval & :: & Expr \rightarrow Int \\
eval\ e & = & eval'\ e\ c1
\end{array}
$$

The next stage in applying defunctionalization is to define a datatype whose values represent the three combinators that we have isolated:

$$
\mathbf{data}\ CONT\ =\ C1 \mid C2\ Expr\ CONT \mid C3\ Int\ CONT
$$

The constructors of this datatype have the same types as the corresponding combinators, except that the new type *CONT* plays the role of *Cont*:

$$
\begin{array}{lll}
C1 & :: & CONT \\
C2 & :: & Expr \rightarrow CONT \rightarrow CONT \\
C3 & :: & Int \rightarrow CONT \rightarrow CONT
\end{array}
$$

The fact that values of type *CONT* represent continuations of type *Cont* can be formalised by defining a function that maps from one to the other:

$$
\begin{array}{lll}
apply & :: & CONT \rightarrow Cont \\
apply\ C1 & = & c1 \\
apply\ (C2\ y\ c) & = & c2\ y\ (apply\ c) \\
apply\ (C3\ n\ c) & = & c3\ n\ (apply\ c)
\end{array}
$$

The name of this function derives from the fact that when its type is expanded to $apply :: CONT \rightarrow Int \rightarrow Int$, it can be viewed as applying a representation of a continuation to an integer to give another integer.

Our aim now is to define a new semantics, $eval''$, that behaves in the same way as our previous semantics, $eval'$, except that it uses values of type *CONT* rather than continuations of type *Cont*. That is, we seek to define a function

$$
eval'' \ :: \ Expr \rightarrow CONT \rightarrow Int
$$

such that:

$$
eval''\ e\ c\ =\ eval'\ e\ (apply\ c)
$$

As previously, we calculate the definition for the function $eval''$ directly from this equation by the use of structural induction on *Expr*.

Case: *Val n*

$$
\begin{array}{l}
eval''\ (Val\ n)\ c \\
= \quad \{\ \text{specification of } eval''\ \} \\
eval'\ (Val\ n)\ (apply\ c) \\
= \quad \{\ \text{definition of } eval'\ \} \\
apply\ c\ n
\end{array}
$$

Case: *Add x y*

> *eval″* (*Add x y*) *c*
> =   { specification of *eval″* }
> *eval′* (*Add x y*) (*apply c*)
> =   { definition of *eval′* }
> *eval′ x* (*c2 y* (*apply c*))
> =   { definition of *apply* }
> *eval′ x* (*apply* (*C2 y c*))
> =   { induction hypothesis for *x* }
> *eval″ x* (*C2 y c*)

In conclusion, we have calculated the following recursive definition:

$$
\begin{array}{lcl}
eval'' & :: & Expr \to CONT \to Int \\
eval''\ (Val\ n)\ c & = & apply\ c\ n \\
eval''\ (Add\ x\ y)\ c & = & eval''\ x\ (C2\ y\ c)
\end{array}
$$

However, the definition for *apply* still refers to the previous semantics *eval′*, via its use of the combinator *c2*. We calculate a new definition for *apply* that refers to our new semantics instead by the use of case analysis on *CONT*.

Case: *C1*

> *apply C1 n*
> =   { definition of *apply* }
> *c1 n*
> =   { definition of *c1* }
> *n*

Case: *C2 y c*

> *apply* (*C2 y c*) *n*
> =   { definition of *apply* }
> *c2 y* (*apply c*) *n*
> =   { definition of *c2* }
> *eval′ y* (*c3 n* (*apply c*))
> =   { definition of *apply* }
> *eval′ y* (*apply* (*C3 n c*))
> =   { specification of *eval″* }
> *eval″ y* (*C3 n c*)

Case: *C3 n c*

> *apply* (*C3 n c*) *m*
> =   { definition of *apply* }
> *c3 n* (*apply c*) *m*
> =   { definition of *c3* }
> *apply c* (*n* + *m*)

In conclusion, we have calculated the following new definition:

$$
\begin{array}{lcl}
apply & :: & CONT \rightarrow Int \rightarrow Int \\
apply\ C1\ n & = & n \\
apply\ (C2\ y\ c)\ n & = & eval''\ y\ (C3\ n\ c) \\
apply\ (C3\ n\ c)\ m & = & apply\ c\ (n+m)
\end{array}
$$

We have now eliminated the use of functions as arguments, and hence made the semantics first-order again. But what about the fact that *eval''* and *apply* are curried functions, and hence return functions as results? As is common practice, we do not view the use of functions as results as being higher-order, as it is not essential and can easily be eliminated if required by uncurrying.

Finally, our original semantics can be recovered from our new semantics by redefining *eval e = eval'' e C1*, as can be verified by a simple calculation:

$$
\begin{array}{ll}
& eval\ e \\
= & \{\ \text{previous definition of } eval\ \} \\
& eval'\ e\ (\lambda n \rightarrow n) \\
= & \{\ \text{definition of } c1\ \} \\
& eval'\ e\ c1 \\
= & \{\ \text{definition of } apply\ \} \\
& eval'\ e\ (apply\ C1) \\
= & \{\ \text{specification of } eval''\ \} \\
& eval''\ e\ C1
\end{array}
$$

Step 3: Refactor

At this point, after making two transformations to the original semantics, the reader may be wondering what we have actually produced? In fact, we now have an abstract machine for evaluating expressions, but this only becomes clear after we *refactor* the definitions, in this simple case by just renaming the components. In detail, we rename *CONT* as *Cont*, *C1* as *STOP*, *C2* as *EVAL*, *C3* as *ADD*, *eval''* as *eval*, *apply* as *exec*, and *eval* as *run* to give the following machine:

$$
\begin{array}{lcl}
\textbf{data}\ Cont & = & STOP \mid EVAL\ Expr\ Cont \mid ADD\ Int\ Cont \\
\\
eval & :: & Expr \rightarrow Cont \rightarrow Int \\
eval\ (Val\ n)\ c & = & exec\ c\ n \\
eval\ (Add\ x\ y)\ c & = & eval\ x\ (EVAL\ y\ c) \\
\\
exec & :: & Cont \rightarrow Int \rightarrow Int \\
exec\ STOP\ n & = & n \\
exec\ (EVAL\ y\ c)\ n & = & eval\ y\ (ADD\ n\ c) \\
exec\ (ADD\ n\ c)\ m & = & exec\ c\ (n+m) \\
\\
run & :: & Expr \rightarrow Int \\
run\ e & = & eval\ e\ STOP
\end{array}
$$

We now explain the four parts of the abstract machine in turn:

- *Cont* is the type of *control stacks* for the machine, containing instructions that determine the behaviour of the machine after evaluating the current expression. The meaning of the three forms of instructions, *STOP*, *EVAL* and *ADD* will be explained shortly. Note that the type of control stacks could itself be refactored as an explicit list of instructions, as follows:

$$\textbf{type } \textit{Cont} \quad = \quad [\textit{Inst}]$$
$$\textbf{data } \textit{Inst} \quad = \quad \textit{ADD Int} \mid \textit{EVAL Expr}$$

However, we prefer the original definition above because it only requires the definition of a single type rather than a pair of types.

- *eval* evaluates an expression in the context of a control stack. If the expression is an integer value, it is already fully evaluated, and we simply execute the control stack using this integer as an argument. If the expression is an addition, we evaluate the first argument, *x*, placing the instruction *EVAL y* on top of the current control stack to indicate that the second argument, *y*, should be evaluated once that of the first argument is completed.

- *exec* executes a control stack in the context of an integer argument. If the stack is empty, represented by the instruction *STOP*, we simply return the integer argument as the result of the execution. If the top of the stack is an instruction *EVAL y*, we evaluate the expression *y*, placing the instruction *ADD n* on top of the remaining stack to indicate that the current integer argument, *n*, should be added together with the result of evaluating *y* once this is completed. Finally, if the top of the stack is an instruction *ADD m*, evaluation of the two arguments of an addition is now complete, and we execute the remaining control stack in the context of the sum of the two resulting integers.

- *run* evaluates an expression to give an integer, by invoking *eval* with the given expression and the empty control stack as arguments.

The fact that our machine uses two mutually recursive functions, *eval* and *exec*, reflects the fact that it has two states, depending upon whether it is being driven by the structure of the expression (*eval*) or the control stack (*exec*). To illustrate the machine, here is how it evaluates $(2+3)+4$:

$$
\begin{array}{rl}
 & \textit{run } (\textit{Add } (\textit{Add } (\textit{Val } 2) (\textit{Val } 3)) (\textit{Val } 4)) \\
= & \textit{eval } (\textit{Add } (\textit{Add } (\textit{Val } 2) (\textit{Val } 3)) (\textit{Val } 4)) \, \textit{STOP} \\
= & \textit{eval } (\textit{Add } (\textit{Val } 2) (\textit{Val } 3)) (\textit{EVAL } (\textit{Val } 4) \, \textit{STOP}) \\
= & \textit{eval } (\textit{Val } 2) (\textit{EVAL } (\textit{Val } 3) (\textit{EVAL } (\textit{Val } 4) \, \textit{STOP})) \\
= & \textit{exec } (\textit{EVAL } (\textit{Val } 3) (\textit{EVAL } (\textit{Val } 4) \, \textit{STOP})) \, 2 \\
= & \textit{eval } (\textit{Val } 3) (\textit{ADD } 2 (\textit{EVAL } (\textit{Val } 4) \, \textit{STOP})) \\
= & \textit{exec } (\textit{ADD } 2 (\textit{EVAL } (\textit{Val } 4) \, \textit{STOP})) \, 3 \\
= & \textit{exec } (\textit{EVAL } (\textit{Val } 4) \, \textit{STOP}) \, 5 \\
= & \textit{eval } (\textit{Val } 4) (\textit{ADD } 5 \, \textit{STOP}) \\
= & \textit{exec } (\textit{ADD } 5 \, \textit{STOP}) \, 4 \\
= & \textit{exec } \textit{STOP } 9 \\
= & 9
\end{array}
$$

Note how the function *eval* proceeds downwards to the leftmost integer in the expression, maintaining a trail of the pending right-hand expressions on the control stack. In turn, the function *exec* then proceeds upwards through the trail, transferring control back to *eval* and performing additions as appropriate.

Readers familiar with Huet's *zipper* data structure for navigating around expressions [Hue97] may find it useful to note that our type *Cont* is a zipper data structure for *Expr*, specialised to the purpose of evaluating expressions. Moreover, this specialised zipper arose naturally here by a process of systematic calculation, and did not require any prior knowledge of this structure.

4.4 ADDING EXCEPTIONS

Now let us extend our language of arithmetic expressions with simple primitives for throwing and catching an exception:

$$\textbf{data } \textit{Expr} \quad = \quad \dots \mid \textit{Throw} \mid \textit{Catch Expr Expr}$$

Informally, *Throw* abandons the current computation and throws an exception, while *Catch x y* behaves as the expression *x* unless it throws an exception, in which case the catch behaves as the *handler* expression *y*. To formalise the meaning of these new primitives, we first recall the *Maybe* type:

$$\textbf{data } \textit{Maybe a} \quad = \quad \textit{Nothing} \mid \textit{Just a}$$

That is, a value of type *Maybe a* is either *Nothing*, which we think of as an exceptional value, or has the form *Just x* for some *x* of type *a*, which we think of as a normal value [Spi90]. Using this type, our original semantics for expressions can be rewritten to take account of exceptions as follows:

$$
\begin{array}{lll}
\textit{eval} & :: & \textit{Expr} \to \textit{Maybe Int} \\
\textit{eval (Val n)} & = & \textit{Just n} \\
\textit{eval (Add x y)} & = & \textbf{case } \textit{eval x} \textbf{ of} \\
& & \quad \textit{Nothing} \to \textit{Nothing} \\
& & \quad \textit{Just n} \to \textbf{case } \textit{eval y} \textbf{ of} \\
& & \qquad \textit{Nothing} \to \textit{Nothing} \\
& & \qquad \textit{Just m} \to \textit{Just } (n+m) \\
\textit{eval (Throw)} & = & \textit{Nothing} \\
\textit{eval (Catch x y)} & = & \textbf{case } \textit{eval x} \textbf{ of} \\
& & \quad \textit{Nothing} \to \textit{eval y} \\
& & \quad \textit{Just n} \to \textit{Just n}
\end{array}
$$

We will now calculate an abstract machine from this extended semantics, by following the same three-step process as previously. That is, we first add continuations, then defunctionalize, and finally refactor the definitions.

Step 1: Add continuations

Because our semantics now returns a result of type *Maybe Int*, the type of continuations that we use must be modified accordingly:

$$\textbf{type } Cont \;\; = \;\; Maybe\ Int \rightarrow Maybe\ Int$$

Our aim now is to define a new semantics

$$eval' \;\; :: \;\; Expr \rightarrow Cont \rightarrow Maybe\ Int$$

such that:

$$eval'\ e\ c \;\; = \;\; c\ (eval\ e)$$

That is, the new semantics behaves in the same way as *eval*, except that it applies a continuation to the result. As previously, we can calculate a recursive definition for *eval'* directly from this equation by structural induction on *Expr*:

$$
\begin{aligned}
eval' \quad &:: \quad Expr \rightarrow Cont \rightarrow Maybe\ Int \\
eval'\ (Val\ n)\ c \quad &= \quad c\ (Just\ n) \\
eval'\ (Throw)\ c \quad &= \quad c\ Nothing \\
eval'\ (Add\ x\ y)\ c \quad &= \quad eval'\ x\ (\lambda x' \rightarrow \textbf{case}\ x'\ \textbf{of} \\
&\qquad Nothing \rightarrow c\ Nothing \\
&\qquad Just\ n \rightarrow eval'\ y\ (\lambda y' \rightarrow \textbf{case}\ y'\ \textbf{of} \\
&\qquad\qquad Nothing \rightarrow c\ Nothing \\
&\qquad\qquad Just\ m \rightarrow c\ (Just\ (n+m))))) \\
eval'\ (Catch\ x\ y)\ c \quad &= \quad eval'\ x\ (\lambda x' \rightarrow \textbf{case}\ x'\ \textbf{of} \\
&\qquad Nothing \rightarrow eval'\ y\ c \\
&\qquad Just\ n \rightarrow c\ (Just\ n))
\end{aligned}
$$

(The above and subsequent omitted calculations are included in the extended version of the article.) In turn, our original semantics can be recovered by invoking our new semantics with the identity continuation. That is, we have

$$
\begin{aligned}
eval \quad &:: \quad Expr \rightarrow Maybe\ Int \\
eval\ e \quad &= \quad eval'\ e\ (\lambda x \rightarrow x)
\end{aligned}
$$

Step 2: Defunctionalize

Our new semantics uses four forms of continuations, namely one to invoke the semantics, two in the case for addition, and one in the case for catch. We define four combinators for constructing these continuations:

$$
\begin{array}{rcl}
c1 & :: & Cont \\
c1 & = & \lambda x \rightarrow x \\
c2 & :: & Expr \rightarrow Cont \rightarrow Cont \\
c2\ y\ c & = & \lambda x' \rightarrow \textbf{case } x' \textbf{ of} \\
& & \quad Nothing \rightarrow c\ Nothing \\
& & \quad Just\ n \rightarrow eval'\ y\ (c3\ n\ c) \\
c3 & :: & Int \rightarrow Cont \rightarrow Cont \\
c3\ n\ c & = & \lambda y' \rightarrow \textbf{case } y' \textbf{ of} \\
& & \quad Nothing \rightarrow c\ Nothing \\
& & \quad Just\ m \rightarrow c\ (Just\ (n+m)) \\
c4 & :: & Expr \rightarrow Cont \rightarrow Cont \\
c4\ y\ c & = & \lambda x' \rightarrow \textbf{case } x' \textbf{ of} \\
& & \quad Nothing \rightarrow eval'\ y\ c \\
& & \quad Just\ n \rightarrow c\ (Just\ n)
\end{array}
$$

Using these combinators, our semantics can now be rewritten as follows:

$$
\begin{array}{rcl}
eval' & :: & Expr \rightarrow Cont \rightarrow Maybe\ Int \\
eval'\ (Val\ n)\ c & = & c\ (Just\ n) \\
eval'\ (Throw)\ c & = & c\ Nothing \\
eval'\ (Add\ x\ y)\ c & = & eval'\ x\ (c2\ y\ c) \\
eval'\ (Catch\ x\ y)\ c & = & eval'\ x\ (c4\ y\ c) \\
eval & :: & Expr \rightarrow Maybe\ Int \\
eval\ e & = & eval'\ e\ c1
\end{array}
$$

We now define a datatype to represent the four combinators, together with an application function that formalises the representation:

$$
\begin{array}{rcl}
\textbf{data } CONT & = & C1 \mid C2\ Expr\ CONT \mid C3\ Int\ Cont \mid C4\ Expr\ CONT \\
apply & :: & CONT \rightarrow Cont \\
apply\ C1 & = & c1 \\
apply\ (C2\ y\ c) & = & c2\ y\ (apply\ c) \\
apply\ (C3\ n\ c) & = & c3\ n\ (apply\ c) \\
apply\ (C4\ y\ c) & = & c4\ y\ (apply\ c)
\end{array}
$$

Our aim now is to define a new semantics

$$eval'' \ :: \ Expr \rightarrow CONT \rightarrow Maybe\ Int$$

such that:

$$eval''\ e\ c \ = \ eval'\ e\ (apply\ c)$$

That is, the new semantics behaves in the same way as $eval'$, except that it uses representations of continuations rather than actual continuations. We can calculate the definition for *eval″* by structural induction on *Expr*:

$$
\begin{aligned}
eval'' & \quad :: \quad Expr \rightarrow CONT \rightarrow Maybe\ Int \\
eval''\ (Val\ n)\ c & \quad = \quad apply\ c\ (Just\ n) \\
eval''\ (Throw)\ c & \quad = \quad apply\ c\ Nothing \\
eval''\ (Add\ x\ y)\ c & \quad = \quad eval''\ x\ (C2\ y\ c) \\
eval''\ (Catch\ x\ y)\ c & \quad = \quad eval''\ x\ (C4\ y\ c)
\end{aligned}
$$

In turn, we can calculate a new definition for *apply* by case analysis:

$$
\begin{aligned}
apply & \quad :: \quad CONT \rightarrow Maybe\ Int \rightarrow Maybe\ Int \\
apply\ C1\ x & \quad = \quad x \\
apply\ (C2\ y\ c)\ Nothing & \quad = \quad apply\ c\ Nothing \\
apply\ (C2\ y\ c)\ (Just\ n) & \quad = \quad eval''\ y\ (C3\ n\ c) \\
apply\ (C3\ n\ c)\ Nothing & \quad = \quad apply\ c\ Nothing \\
apply\ (C3\ n\ c)\ (Just\ m) & \quad = \quad apply\ c\ (Just\ (n+m)) \\
apply\ (C4\ y\ c)\ Nothing & \quad = \quad eval''\ y\ c \\
apply\ (C4\ y\ c)\ (Just\ n) & \quad = \quad apply\ c\ (Just\ n)
\end{aligned}
$$

Our original semantics can be recovered by invoking our new semantics with the representation of the identity continuation:

$$
\begin{aligned}
eval & \quad :: \quad Expr \rightarrow Maybe\ Int \\
eval & \quad = \quad eval''\ e\ C1
\end{aligned}
$$

Step 3: Refactor

We now rename the components in the same way as previously, and rename the new combinator *C4* as *HAND*. This time around, however, refactoring amounts to more than just renaming. In particular, we split the application function

$$
apply \quad :: \quad Cont \rightarrow Maybe\ Int \rightarrow Maybe\ Int
$$

into two separate application functions

$$
\begin{aligned}
exec & \quad :: \quad Cont \rightarrow Int \rightarrow Maybe\ Int \\
unwind & \quad :: \quad Cont \rightarrow Maybe\ Int
\end{aligned}
$$

such that:

$$
\begin{aligned}
apply\ c\ (Just\ n) & \quad = \quad exec\ c\ n \\
apply\ c\ Nothing & \quad = \quad unwind\ c
\end{aligned}
$$

That is, *exec* deals with normal arguments, and *unwind* with exceptional arguments. We can calculate the definitions for *exec* and *unwind* by structural induction on *Cont*, as a result of which we obtain the following machine:

data *Cont*	=	*STOP* | *EVAL Expr Cont* |
		ADD Int Cont | *HAND Expr Cont*
eval	::	*Expr → Cont → Maybe Int*
eval (*Val n*) *c*	=	*exec c n*
eval (*Throw*) *c*	=	*unwind c*
eval (*Add x y*) *c*	=	*eval x* (*EVAL y c*)
eval (*Catch x y*) *c*	=	*eval x* (*HAND y c*)
exec	::	*Cont → Int → Maybe Int*
exec STOP n	=	*Just n*
exec (*EVAL y c*) *n*	=	*eval y* (*ADD n c*)
exec (*ADD n c*) *m*	=	*exec c* (*n + m*)
exec (*HAND _ c*) *n*	=	*exec c n*
unwind	::	*Cont → Maybe Int*
unwind STOP	=	*Nothing*
unwind (*EVAL _ c*)	=	*unwind c*
unwind (*ADD _ c*)	=	*unwind c*
unwind (*HAND y c*)	=	*eval y c*
run	::	*Expr → Maybe Int*
run e	=	*eval e STOP*

We now explain the three main functions of the abstract machine:

- *eval* evaluates an expression in the context of a control stack. The cases for integer values and addition are as previously. If the expression is a throw, we *unwind the stack* seeking a handler expression. If the expression is a catch, we evaluate its first argument, *x*, and *mark the stack* with the instruction *HAND y* to indicate that its second argument, the handler *y*, should be used if evaluation of its first produces an exceptional value.

- *exec* executes a control stack in the context of an integer argument. The first three cases are as previously, except that if the stack is empty the resulting integer is tagged as a normal result value. If the top of the stack is a handler instruction, there is no need for the associated handler expression because a normal integer result has already been produced, and we *unmark the stack* by popping the handler and then continue executing.

- *unwind* executes the control stack in the context of an exception. If the stack is empty, the exception is uncaught and we simply return the exceptional result value. If the top of the stack is an evaluation or an addition instruction, there is no need for their arguments because a handler is being sought, and we pop them from the stack and then continue unwinding. If the top of the stack is a handler instruction, we catch the exception by evaluating the associated handler expression in the context of the remaining stack.

Note that the idea of marking, unmarking, and unwinding the stack arose directly from the calculations, and did not require any prior knowledge of these concepts. It is also interesting to note that the above machine produced by calculation is both simpler and more efficient that those we had previously designed by hand. In particular, our previous machines did not make a clean separation between the three concepts of evaluating an expression (*eval*), executing the control stack (*exec*) and unwinding the control stack (*unwind*).

To illustrate our machine, here is how it evaluates $1 + (catch\ (2 + throw)\ 3)$:

$$
\begin{aligned}
& run\ (Add\ (Val\ 1)\ (Catch\ (Add\ (Val\ 2)\ Throw)\ (Val\ 3))) \\
= \ & eval\ (Add\ (Val\ 1)\ (Catch\ (Add\ (Val\ 2)\ Throw)\ (Val\ 3)))\ STOP \\
= \ & eval\ (Val\ 1)\ (EVAL\ (Catch\ (Add\ (Val\ 2)\ Throw)\ (Val\ 3))\ STOP) \\
= \ & exec\ (EVAL\ (Catch\ (Add\ (Val\ 2)\ Throw)\ (Val\ 3))\ STOP)\ 1 \\
= \ & eval\ (Catch\ (Add\ (Val\ 2)\ Throw)\ (Val\ 3))\ (ADD\ 1\ STOP) \\
= \ & eval\ (Add\ (Val\ 2)\ Throw)\ (HAND\ (Val\ 3)\ (ADD\ 1\ STOP)) \\
= \ & eval\ (Val\ 2)\ (EVAL\ Throw\ (HAND\ (Val\ 3)\ (ADD\ 1\ STOP))) \\
= \ & exec\ (EVAL\ Throw\ (HAND\ (Val\ 3)\ (ADD\ 1\ STOP)))\ 2 \\
= \ & eval\ Throw\ (ADD\ 2\ (HAND\ (Val\ 3)\ (ADD\ 1\ STOP))) \\
= \ & unwind\ (ADD\ 2\ (HAND\ (Val\ 3)\ (ADD\ 1\ STOP))) \\
= \ & unwind\ (HAND\ (Val\ 3)\ (ADD\ 1\ STOP)) \\
= \ & eval\ (Val\ 3)\ (ADD\ 1\ STOP) \\
= \ & exec\ (ADD\ 1\ STOP)\ 3 \\
= \ & exec\ STOP\ 4 \\
= \ & 4
\end{aligned}
$$

That is, the machine first proceeds normally by transferring control back and forward between the functions *eval* and *exec*, until the exception is encountered, at which point the control stack is unwound to find the handler expression, and the machine then proceeds normally once again.

4.5 FURTHER WORK

We have shown how an abstract machine for a small language with exceptions can be calculated in a systematic way from a semantics for the language, using a three-step process of adding continuations, defunctionalizing, and refactoring. Moreover, the calculations themselves are straightforward, only requiring the basic concepts of structural induction and case analysis.

Possible directions for further work include exploring the impact of higher-level algebraic methods (such as monads [Wad92] and folds [Hut99]) on the calculations, mechanically checking the calculations using a theorem proving system (for example, see [Nip04]), factorising the abstract machine into the composition of a compiler and a virtual machine [ABDM03a], and generalising the underlying language (we are particularly interested in the addition of interrupts).

Acknowledgements. Thanks to the referees, Thorsten Altenkirch, Olivier Danvy, Conor McBride, and the WG2.1 meeting in Nottingham for useful comments.

REFERENCES

[ABDM03a] Mads Sig Ager, Dariusz Biernacki, Olivier Danvy, and Jan Midtgaard. From Interpreter to Compiler and Virtual Machine: a Functional Derivation. Technical Report RS-03-14, BRICS, Aarhus, Denmark, March 2003.

[ABDM03b] Mads Sig Ager, Dariusz Biernacki, Olivier Danvy, and Jan Midtgaard. A functional correspondence between evaluators and abstract machines. In *Proceedings of the Fifth ACM-SIGPLAN International Conference on Principles and Practice of Declarative Programming*, pages 8–19, Uppsala, Sweden, 2003. ACM Press, New York.

[ADM04] Mads Sig Ager, Olivier Danvy, and Jan Midtgaard. A functional correspondence between monadic evaluators and abstract machines for languages with computational effects. Research Series RS-04-28, BRICS, Department of Computer Science, University of Aarhus, December 2004.

[Bac03] Roland Backhouse. *Program Construction: Calculating Implementations from Specifications*. John Wiley, 2003.

[DN01] Olivier Danvy and Lasse R. Nielsen. Defunctionalization at work. In *Proceedings of the Third ACM-SIGPLAN International Conference on Principles and Practice of Declarative Programming*, pages 162–174, Firenze, September 2001. ACM Press, New York.

[Hue97] Gerard Huet. The Zipper. *Journal of Functional Programming*, 7(5):549–554, September 1997.

[Hut99] Graham Hutton. A Tutorial on the Universality and Expressiveness of Fold. *Journal of Functional Programming*, 9(4):355–372, July 1999.

[HW04] Graham Hutton and Joel Wright. Compiling Exceptions Correctly. In *Proceedings of the 7th International Conference on Mathematics of Program Construction*, volume 3125 of *Lecture Notes in Computer Science*, Stirling, Scotland, July 2004. Springer, Berlin.

[Lan64] Peter Landin. The mechanical evaluation of expressions. *The Computer Journal*, 6(4):308–320, 1964.

[Mei92] Erik Meijer. *Calculating Compilers*. PhD thesis, University of Nijmegen, 1992.

[Nip04] Tobias Nipkow. Compiling Exceptions Correctly. In *Archive of Formal Proofs*. 2004. Available from http://afp.sourceforge.net/.

[Pey03] Simon Peyton Jones. *Haskell 98 Language and Libraries: The Revised Report*. Cambridge University Press, 2003.

[Rey72] John C. Reynolds. Definitional Interpreters for Higher-Order Programming Languages. In *Proceedings of the ACM annual conference*, pages 717–740. ACM Press, 1972.

[Spi90] Mike Spivey. A Functional Theory of Exceptions. *Science of Computer Programming*, 14(1):25–43, 1990.

[Wad92] Philip Wadler. The Essence of Functional Programming. In *Proc. Principles of Programming Languages*, 1992.

Chapter 5

Generalizing the AUGMENT Combinator

Neil Ghani[1], Tarmo Uustalu[2], and Varmo Vene[3]

Abstract: The usual initial algebra semantics of inductive types provides a clear and uniform explanation for the FOLD combinator. In an APLAS 2004 paper [GUV04], we described an alternative equivalent semantics of inductive types as limits of algebra structure forgetting functors. This gave us an elegant universal property based account of the BUILD and AUGMENT combinators, which form the core of the shortcut deforestation program transformation method by Gill et al. [GLP93, Gil96]. Here we present further evidence for the flexibility of our approach by showing that a useful AUGMENT-like combinator is definable for a far wider class of parameterized inductive types than free monads, namely for all monads arising from a parameterized monad via an initial algebra construction.

5.1 INTRODUCTION

The standard approach to programming with inductive types is based on the IN/FOLD (constructors/structural recursion) syntax derived directly from their initial algebra semantics. This encourages a modular style of programming where functions are composed of simpler functions using intermediate data structures as a glue. Apart from the obvious advantages for the programmer, the use of intermediate data structures, which have to be constructed, traversed and discarded, can make programs inefficient both in terms of time and space. This calls for methods for transforming a modular program into an equivalent but more efficient program where these intermediate structures have been eliminated.

[1]Dept. of Math. and Comp. Sci., University of Leicester, University Road, Leicester, LE1 7RH, UK; E-mail: `N.Ghani@mcs.le.ac.uk`

[2]Institute of Cybernetics, Tallinn Univ. of Technology, Akadeemia tee 21, EE-12618 Tallinn, Estonia; E-mail: `tarmo@cs.ioc.ee`

[3]Dept. of Computer Science, University of Tartu, Liivi 2, EE-50409 Tartu, Estonia; E-mail: `varmo@cs.ut.ee`

One of the most successful methods for eliminating intermediate data structures has been shortcut deforestation, originally introduced by Gill et al. [GLP93, Gil96] for lists and generalized for other inductive types by Launchbury and Sheard and Takano and Meyer [LS95, TM95]. This is based on the interaction of FOLD with a novel constructor combinator BUILD, capturing uniform production of data structures in a fashion matching the consumption pattern of FOLD. Deforestation happens by repeated application of a simple transformation rule of FOLD/BUILD fusion. Gill [Gil96] also introduced an enhanced AUGMENT combinator for lists and Johann [Joh02] generalized it for arbitrary inductive types with distinguished non-recursive constructors (so that list types and their nil constructors became instances).

Despite the success of the shortcut deforestation method, its theoretical explanations (see for example [TM95]) have not been fully satisfactory, typically relying on informal uses of Wadler's [Wad89] free theorems, without discussing the exact conditions under which these are available. It is only recently that Johann [Joh03, Joh02] has proved the correctness of FOLD/BUILD and FOLD/AUGMENT fusion via parametricity of contextual equivalence. In an APLAS 2004 paper [GUV04], we approached the issue from a different perspective. We set out to give a language-independent axiomatic specification of BUILD and AUGMENT and derived it from an elementary alternative semantics of inductive types as limits of algebra structure forgetting functors. That semantics has BUILD rather than IN as the basic constructor of an inductive type and explains also the impredicative encoding of inductive types.

This short paper is a companion paper to [GUV04]. We present further evidence for the merits of the transparency of our framework by deriving a strong generalization of the AUGMENT combinator. We observe that AUGMENT is a monadic operation and show that AUGMENT is definable not only for free monads, which is essentially what Johann's version [Joh02] amounts to, but far more generally for any monad arising from a parameterized monad via the initial algebras based construction of Uustalu [Uus03]. The extension operation of such monads can be seen as a grafting operation. The FOLD/AUGMENT fusion rule makes it possible to deforest programs involving this form of grafting.

The paper is organized as follows. In Sections 2, 3 we give a very condensed motivation for BUILD and AUGMENT combinators and review the account of FOLD/BUILD and AUGMENT from [GUV04]. In Section 4, which is the main section, we extend this account to the generalized version AUGMENT, to conclude in Section 5.

We use Haskell in our examples, because its syntax is familiar to many, but this is purely illustrative. We are by no means asserting that Haskell's polymorphism is fully compliant with the parametricity requirements imposed by our semantics.

5.2 SEMANTICS OF FOLD/BUILD

Traditionally, the inductive type determined by an endofunctor F on a semantic category C is modelled by a chosen initial F-algebra. Such a characterization via a universal property immediately suggests a syntax and a theory for programming with the type in question and for reasoning about it. The initial algebra semantics gives us the familiar IN/FOLD syntax and theory, see for example [Hag87]. Indeed, by introducing the notations $(\mu F, \text{in}_F)$ for the initial F-algebra and $\text{fold}_{F,C}\varphi$ for the unique map to an F-algebra (X, φ), we institute a type μF (the inductive type) equipped with a constructor in_F and a destructor fold_F (the corresponding structural recursor) with the typing rules

$$\text{in}_F : F(\mu F) \to \mu F \qquad \frac{(X, \varphi) \in F\text{-}\mathbf{alg}}{\text{fold}_{F,X}\varphi : \mu F \to X}$$

β-conversion rule

$$\frac{(X, \varphi) \in F\text{-}\mathbf{alg}}{\text{fold}_{F,X}\varphi \circ \text{in}_F = \varphi \circ F\text{fold}_{F,X}\varphi}$$

and η- and permutative conversion rules

$$\text{fold}_{F,\mu F}\text{in}_F = \text{id}_{\mu F} \qquad \frac{f : (X, \varphi) \to (Y, \psi) \in F\text{-}\mathbf{alg}}{f \circ \text{fold}_{F,X}\varphi = \text{fold}_{F,Y}\psi}$$

As a well-known example, lists over type A arise as the initial algebra of the functor $1 + A \times -$. The Haskell Prelude introduces the (parameterized) type of lists and equips it with IN/FOLD syntax as follows, the β-rule defining the computational behavior of the FOLD combinator.

```
data [a] = [] | a : [a]

foldr :: (a -> x -> x) -> x -> [a] -> x
foldr c n [] = n
foldr c n (a : as) = c a (foldr c n as)
```

In shortcut deforestation, however, one uses a different syntax: producers of lists must be presented as applications of a BUILD combinator

```
build :: (forall x. (a -> x -> x) -> x -> x) -> [a]
build theta = theta (:) []
```

The merit is that applications of FOLD can be cancelled by those of BUILD as described by the so-called FOLD/BUILD fusion law

```
foldr c n (build theta) == theta c n
```

In [GUV04], we motivated this different syntax by showing that the inductive type given by F can alternatively be interpreted as a chosen limit of the functor $U_F : F\text{-}\mathbf{alg} \to C$. By definition, a U_F-cone is an object C in C and, for any F-algebra (X, φ), a map $\Theta_X\varphi : C \to X$ in C, such that (*) for any F-algebra map $f : (X, \varphi) \to (Y, \psi)$, we have $f \circ \Theta_X\varphi = \Theta_Y\psi$. A U_F-cone map $h : (C, \Theta) \to (D, \Xi)$ is a map $h : C \to D$ in C such that, for any F-algebra (X, φ), we have $\Xi_X\varphi \circ h = \Theta_X\varphi$. A U_F-limit is a U_F-cone to which there is a unique map from any other

U_F-cone. Writing $(\mu^*F, \mathsf{fold}_F^*)$ for the U_F-limit (in case it exists) and $\mathsf{build}_{F,C}^*\Theta$ for the unique map from a U_F-cone (C,Θ), we obtain a type μ^*F with a destructor fold_F^* and a constructor build_F^* governed by the typing rules

$$\frac{(X,\varphi) \in F\text{-}\mathbf{alg}}{\mathsf{fold}_{F,X}^*\varphi : \mu^*F \to X} \qquad \frac{f : (X,\varphi) \to (Y,\psi) \in F\text{-}\mathbf{alg}}{f \circ \mathsf{fold}_{F,X}^*\varphi = \mathsf{fold}_{F,Y}^*\psi} \qquad \frac{(C,\Theta) \in U_F\text{-}\mathbf{cone}}{\mathsf{build}_{F,C}^*\Theta : C \to \mu^*F}$$

The corresponding β-conversion rule is

$$\frac{(C,\Theta) \in U_F\text{-}\mathbf{cone} \quad (X,\varphi) \in F\text{-}\mathbf{alg}}{\mathsf{fold}_{F,X}^*\varphi \circ \mathsf{build}_{F,C}^*\Theta = \Theta_X\varphi}$$

and the η- and permutative conversion rules are

$$\mathsf{id}_{\mu^*F} = \mathsf{build}_{F,\mu^*F}^*\mathsf{fold}_F^* \qquad \frac{h : (C,\Theta) \to (D,\Xi) \in U_F\text{-}\mathbf{cone}}{\mathsf{build}_{F,D}^*\Xi \circ h = \mathsf{build}_{F,C}^*\Theta}$$

Inspecting these rules, one sees immediately that fold_F^* and build_F^* type exactly as FOLD and BUILD should, although with the reservation that the argument of build_F^* is required to meet the coherence condition (*). Moreover, the β-conversion rule is axiomatic FOLD/BUILD fusion. This makes the limit of forgetful functor semantics an appealing candidate justification for the FOLD/BUILD syntax (with BUILD rather than IN as the primitive constructor) and for the fusion rule. Remarkably, the condition (*) crisply explicates the kind of parametricity of polymorphism that is required for everything to work.

That the alternative semantics is adequate by being equivalent to the standard one is demonstrated by the following proposition.

Proposition 5.1. *Let C be a category and $F : C \to C$ be a functor. (a) If there is an initial F-algebra $(\mu F, \mathsf{in}_F)$, then μF is the vertex of a U_F-limit. (b) If there is a U_F-limit $(\mu^*F, \mathsf{fold}_F^*)$, then μ^*F is the carrier of an initial F-algebra.*

Proof (constructions). (a) Set, for any U_F-cone (C,Θ), $\mathsf{build}_{F,C}\Theta =_{\mathrm{df}} \Theta_{\mu F}\mathsf{in}_F$; $(\mu F, \mathsf{fold}_F)$ is a U_F-cone and $\mathsf{build}_{F,C}\Theta$ a unique map from any U_F-cone.

(b) Set, for any F-algebra (X,φ), $\mathsf{infold}_{F,X}^*\varphi =_{\mathrm{df}} \varphi \circ F\mathsf{fold}_{F,X}^*\varphi$; set $\mathsf{in}_F^* =_{\mathrm{df}} \mathsf{build}_{F,F(\mu^*F)}^*\mathsf{infold}_F^*$; $(\mu^*F, \mathsf{in}_F^*)$ is an F-algebra and $\mathsf{fold}_{F,X}^*\varphi$ is a unique map to any F-algebra (X,φ). $\square$

The condition (*) turns out to be equivalent to a strong dinaturality condition.

Definition 5.1. *Let $H, K : C^{\mathrm{op}} \times C \to \mathcal{D}$ be functors. A strongly dinatural transformation $\Theta : H \to K$ is a family of maps $\Theta_X : H(X,X) \to K(X,X)$ in $\mathcal{D}$ for all objects X in C such that, for every map $f : X \to Y$ in C, object W and maps $p_0 : W \to H(X,X)$, $p_1 : W \to H(Y,Y)$ in $\mathcal{D}$, if the square in the following diagram* *commutes, then so does the hexagon:*

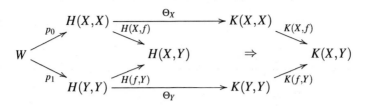

Proposition 5.2. *Let C be a locally small category and $F : C \to C$ a functor. A U_F-cone structure with vertex C is the same thing as a strong dinatural transformation from $\mathrm{Hom}(F-,-)$ to $\mathrm{Hom}(C,-)$.*

The relevance of this proposition for programming languages is that the coherence condition (*) is for free whenever strong dinaturality is.

5.3 THE AUGMENT OF FREE MONADS

BUILD presentations of producers do not always suffice for shortcut deforestation. A prototypical example for lists is the append function

```
append as bs = foldr (:) bs as
```

The definition as a BUILD

```
append as bs = build (\ c n -> foldr c (foldr c n bs) as)
```

introduces an unnatural traversal of the list appended and this traversal is not necessarily removed in shortcut deforestation.

The solution proposed by Gill [Gil96] consists in deploying an enhanced version of BUILD, called AUGMENT. For lists, the Haskell version of this combinator is the following:

```
augment :: (forall x. (a -> x -> x) -> x -> x) -> [a] -> [a]
augment theta bs = theta (:) bs
```

An AUGMENT represents nothing else than a BUILD followed by an append:

```
augment theta bs == append (build theta) bs
```

And conversely, a BUILD is just an AUGMENT applied to nil:

```
build theta == augment theta []
```

But the reason to introduce AUGMENT is that it obeys a special law of fusion with FOLD:

```
foldr c n (augment theta bs) == theta c (foldr c n bs)
```

This law is similar by its spirit to the FOLD/BUILD law. But differently from a BUILD, an AUGMENT does not cancel a FOLD completely: the reduct contains a residual FOLD.

The definition of the append function as an AUGMENT is

```
append as bs = augment (\ c n -> foldr c n as) bs
```

A similar AUGMENT combinator can be easily defined for arbitrary inductive types with non-recursive constructors to obtain a version of shortcut deforestation tailored specifically for producer functions that perform grafting, see Johann [Joh02]. In [GUV04], we justified a slightly more general version in the style our FOLD/BUILD account and, in line with our general methodology, derived it from a unique existence situation. In that version, AUGMENT combinators are associated to free monads, which are families of inductive types rather than single inductive types.

Recall that a *monad* (in *extension form*) on a category C is an object mapping $T : |C| \to |C|$ together with, for any object A, a map $\eta_A : A \to TA$ (*unit*), and for any map $f : A \to TB$, a map $f^* : TA \to TB$ (*extension operation*) such that (i) for any map $f : A \to TB$, $f^* \circ \eta_A = f$, (ii) for any object A, $\eta_A{}^* = \mathrm{id}_{TA}$, and (iii) for any maps $f : A \to TB$, $g : B \to TC$, $(g^* \circ f)^* = g^* \circ f^*$.

Recall also that monads in Haskell are implemented via a type constructor class:

```
class Monad m where
  return :: a -> m a
  (>>=) :: m a -> (a -> m b) -> m b
```

The Haskell jargon for the extension operation is 'bind'.

Consider an endofunctor H on a category C and let $T' : C \to [C, C]$ be the functor given by $T'AX =_{df} A + HX$. Then, if an initial $T'A$-algebra (= a free H-algebra over A) exists for every object A of C, we can get a functor $T : C \to C$ by defining $TA =_{df} \mu(T'A)$. This models an inductive type parameterized in non-recursive constructors. Decompose each map $\mathsf{in}_{T'A}$ into two maps $\eta_A : A \to TA$ and $\tau_A : H(TA) \to TA$ by setting

$$\eta_A \quad =_{df} \quad \mathsf{in}_{T'A} \circ \mathsf{inl}_{A,H(TA)}$$
$$\tau_A \quad =_{df} \quad \mathsf{in}_{T'A} \circ \mathsf{inr}_{A,H(TA)}$$

Define, finally, for any map $f : A \to TB$, a map $f^* : TA \to TB$ by

$$f^* =_{df} \mathsf{fold}_{T'A,TB}[f, \tau_B]$$

Conceptually, η packages the non-recursive constructors of the parameterized type, τ packages the recursive constructors, and $()^*$ is substitution for non-recursive constructors.

It is standard knowledge the data $(T, \eta, ()^*)$ so constructed constitute a monad which, more specifically, is the free monad generated by the functor H.

The following proposition supplies the parameterized inductive type T with an AUGMENT combinator.

Proposition 5.3. *Let C be a category, $H : C \to C$ a functor such that initial algebras of all functors $T'A =_{df} A + H-$ exist. Let T, η, τ, $()^\star$ be defined as above. Then, for any map $f : A \to TB$ and $U_{T'A}$-cone (C, Θ) there exists a unique map $h : C \to TB$ such that, for any $T'B$-algebra $(X, [\varphi_0, \varphi_1])$, it holds that*

$$\mathsf{fold}_{T'B,X}[\varphi_0, \varphi_1] \circ h = \Theta_X ([\mathsf{fold}_{T'B,X}[\varphi_0, \varphi_1] \circ f, \varphi_1])$$

We denote the unique map by $\mathsf{augment}_{T',C}(\Theta, f)$.

On the level of syntax, the proposition justifies the introduction of a constructor combinator $\mathsf{augment}_{T'}$ with a typing rule

$$\frac{(C, \Theta) \in U_{T'A}\text{-}\mathbf{cone} \quad f : A \to TB}{\mathsf{augment}_{T',C}(\Theta, f) : C \to TB}$$

and β-conversion rule

$$\frac{(C, \Theta) \in U_{T'A}\text{-}\mathbf{cone} \quad f : A \to TB \quad (X, [\varphi_0, \varphi_1]) \in T'B\text{-}\mathbf{alg}}{\mathsf{fold}_{T'B,X}[\varphi_0, \varphi_1] \circ \mathsf{augment}_{T',C}(\Theta, f) = \Theta_X[\mathsf{fold}_{T'B,X}[\varphi_0, \varphi_1] \circ f, \varphi_1]}$$

which is fusion of FOLD and AUGMENT. One also gets a number of conversion rules pertaining to the monad structure on T, some of which we will list in the next section.

The combinator of Johann [Joh02] differs from our version by having the type of non-recursive constructors fixed (so that $B = A$), thus confining the action of the combinator to a single inductive type rather than a family one would obtain by letting the type of non-recursive constructors to vary. (The reason must be that, in the prototypical case of lists, the type of non-recursive constructors is constantly 1; normally, one does not consider the possibility of supporting multiple nil's drawn from a parameter type.) Unfortunately, this restriction hides the important role that the monad structure on T plays in the construction. This role is central for our generalization in the next section.

A typical example of a free monad is the parameterized type of binary leaf labelled trees. Binary leaf labelled trees with leaf label type A are the initial algebra of the functor $A + - \times -$. They are Haskell-implementable as follows:

```
data BLTree a = Leaf a | Bin (BLTree a) (BLTree a)

foldB :: (a -> x) -> (x -> x -> x) -> BLTree a -> x
foldB l b (Leaf a) = l a
foldB l b (Bin as0 as1) = b (foldB l b as0) (foldB l b as1)

instance Monad BLTree where
  return a = Leaf a
  as >>= f = foldB f Bin as
```

The BUILD and AUGMENT combinators are implementable as follows:

```
buildB :: (forall x. (a -> x) -> (x -> x -> x) -> x)
```

```
                                                   -> BLTree a
buildB theta = theta Leaf Bin

augmentB :: (forall x. (a -> x) -> (x -> x -> x) -> x)
                           -> (a -> BLTree b) -> BLTree b
augmentB theta f = theta f Bin
```

The shortcut deforestation laws say that

```
foldB l b (buildB theta) == theta l b
foldB l b (augmentB theta f) == theta (foldB l b . f) b
```

It is also possible to give a generic implementation of the AUGMENT combinator of free monads that caters for all possible shapes of leaf-labelled trees at one go. The code is nearly identical to what we have just seen.

We observe that AUGMENT combinators are about uniform production of inductive data in combination with grafting. Grafting presupposes monadic structure. We have seen that an AUGMENT combinator can be defined for any free monad. But there exist parameterized inductive types carrying a non-free monad structure! Could it be that an AUGMENT-like combinator subject to a fusion law is definable for some of them too? We will answer this question affirmatively in the next section.

5.4 A GENERALIZED AUGMENT COMBINATOR

The AUGMENT combinator for the monad of the free algebras of a functor (or, in other words, the free monad) is a meaningful combinator obeying a useful FOLD/AUGMENT fusion rule, but it is not as general as possible. As we will now show, a similar combinator is possible for any monad obtained from a parameterized monad via initial algebras as described by Uustalu [Uus03]. This generalization is, to our knowledge, entirely new.

We must start by reviewing the construction in [Uus03].

A *parameterized monad* is an object mapping $T' : |C| \to |[C,C]|$ together with, for any objects A, X, a map $\eta'_{A,X} : A \to T'AX$ and, for any map $f : A \to T'BX$, a map $f^\circ : T'AX \to T'BX$ such that (i') for any map $f : A \to T'BX$, $f^\circ \circ \eta'_{A,X} = f$, (ii') for any objects A, X, $(\eta'_{A,X})^\circ = \mathrm{id}_{T'AX}$, (iii') for any maps $f : A \to T'BX$, $g : B \to T'CX$, $(g^\circ \circ f)^\circ = g^\circ \circ f^\circ$, (iv') for any object A and map $\xi : X \to Y$, $T'A\xi \circ \eta'_{A,X} = \eta'_{A,Y}$, and (v') for any maps $f : A \to T'BX$, $\xi : X \to Y$, $T'B\xi \circ f^\circ = (T'B\xi \circ f)^\circ \circ T'A\xi$. It is easy to verify that a parameterized monad on C is essentially just a functor from C to the category **Monad**(C) of monads on C, but we adopt the above presentation as this will be more convenient.

Now if $(T',\eta',()^\circ)$ is a parameterized monad on C, we can consider the initial algebras $(TA,\alpha_A) =_{\mathrm{df}} (\mu(T'A), \mathrm{in}_{T'A})$, provided all functors $T'A$ have an initial algebra. Define, for any object A, a map $\eta_A : A \to TA$ by

$$\eta_A =_{\mathrm{df}} \alpha_A \circ \eta'_{A,TA}$$

and, for any map $f : A \rightarrow TB$, a map $f^\star : TA \rightarrow TB$ by

$$f^\star =_{\mathrm{df}} \mathrm{fold}_{T'A,TB} \left(\alpha_B \circ (\alpha_B^{-1} \circ f)^\circ \right)$$

By a proposition in [Uus03], $(T, \eta, ()^\star)$ is a monad. Its extension operation $()^\star$ is, in a meaningful but very liberal sense, a grafting operation.

Below are some examples of monads arising from parameterized monads in the manner just described:

- The monad of the free algebras of a given functor $H : C \rightarrow C$ (the free monad generated by H). This is the example we already saw: the inducing parameterized monad T' is defined by $T'AX =_{\mathrm{df}} A + HX$ (so that, for any type X, $T'-X$ is the exceptions monad with exceptions type HX).

- The monad of finitely branching node labelled trees (rose trees). The inducing parameterized monad T' is defined by $T'AX =_{\mathrm{df}} A \times \mathrm{List}X$. Notice that in this type of trees values are stored at inner nodes, not at leaves, so substitution must be a bit unusual. The substitution function $f^\star : TA \rightarrow TB$ that corresponds to a given substitution rule $f : A \rightarrow TB$ is specified by the equation

$$f^\star(x[t_1, \ldots t_n]) =_{\mathrm{df}} y[s_1, \ldots, s_m, f^\star(t_1), \ldots, f^\star(t_n)] \text{ where } f(x) =_{\mathrm{df}} y[s_1, \ldots, s_m]$$

- The monad of inductive hyperfunctions [KLP01] with a fixed domain. The inducing parameterized monad T' is defined by $T'AX =_{\mathrm{df}} (X \Rightarrow E) \Rightarrow A$ where E is a fixed object of C.

- A further interesting monad is obtained from the parameterized monad T' defined by $T'AX =_{\mathrm{df}} \mathrm{List}(A + X)$. The bind operation of this monad is defined in terms of the bind operation of the lists monad.

Now, as promised, we can introduce an AUGMENT combinator can for all monads that arise from a parameterized monad in the fashion described above. This results again from a uniquely satisfied property.

Proposition 5.4. *Let* C *be a category and* $(T', \eta', ()^\circ)$ *a parameterized monad on it such that initial algebras of all functors* $T'A$ *exist. Let* T η, τ, $()^\star$ *be defined as above. Then, for any map* $f : A \rightarrow TB$ *and* $U_{T'A}$*-cone* (C, Θ) *there exists a unique map* $h : C \rightarrow TB$ *such that, for any* $T'B$*-algebra* (X, φ), *it holds that*

$$\mathrm{fold}_{T'B,X} \varphi \circ h = \Theta_X \left(\varphi \circ (T'B (\mathrm{fold}_{T'B,X} \varphi) \circ \alpha_B^{-1} \circ f)^\circ \right)$$

As earlier, we denote the unique map by $\mathrm{augment}_{T',C}(\Theta, f)$.

Proof. We prove that

$$\mathrm{augment}_{T',C}(\Theta, f) = \Theta_{TB} \left(\alpha_B \circ (\alpha_B^{-1} \circ f)^\circ \right)$$

For any $T'B$-algebra (X, φ), making use of the axiom (v') of parameterized monads, we have

$$
\begin{aligned}
&\mathsf{fold}_{T'B,X}\, \varphi \circ \alpha_B \circ (\alpha_B^{-1} \circ f)^\circ \\
&= \quad \varphi \circ T'B\,(\mathsf{fold}_{T'B,X}\, \varphi) \circ (\alpha_B^{-1} \circ f)^\circ \\
&= \quad \varphi \circ (T'B\,(\mathsf{fold}_{T'B,X}\, \varphi) \circ \alpha_B^{-1} \circ f)^\circ \circ T'A\,(\mathsf{fold}_{T'B,X}\, \varphi)
\end{aligned}
$$

Hence, $\mathsf{fold}_{T'B,X}\, \varphi$ is a $T'A$-algebra map from $(TB, \alpha_B \circ (\alpha_B^{-1} \circ f)^\circ)$ to $(X, \varphi \circ (T'B\,(\mathsf{fold}_{T'B,X}\, \varphi) \circ \alpha_B^{-1} \circ f)^\circ)$. Hence by (C, Θ) being a $U_{T'A}$-cone

$$
\mathsf{fold}_{T'B,X}\, \varphi \circ \Theta_{TB}\,(\alpha_B \circ (\alpha_B^{-1} \circ f)^\circ) = \Theta_X\,(\varphi \circ (T'B\,(\mathsf{fold}_{T'B,X}\, \varphi) \circ \alpha_B^{-1} \circ f)^\circ)
$$

as needed.

Assume now we have a map $h : C \to TB$ such that, for any $T'B$-algebra (X, φ),

$$
\mathsf{fold}_{T'B,X}\, \varphi \circ h = \Theta_X\,(\varphi \circ (T'B\,(\mathsf{fold}_{T'B,X}\, \varphi) \circ \alpha_B^{-1} \circ f)^\circ)
$$

Then

$$
\begin{aligned}
h &= \quad \mathsf{fold}_{T'B,TB}\, \alpha_B \circ h \\
&= \quad \Theta_{TB}\,(\alpha_B \circ (T'B\,(\mathsf{fold}_{T'B,TB}\, \alpha_B) \circ \alpha_B^{-1} \circ f)^\circ) \\
&= \quad \Theta_{TB}\,(\alpha_B \circ (\alpha_B^{-1} \circ f)^\circ)
\end{aligned}
$$

which completes the proof of uniqueness. $\square$

This unique existence motivates a combinator $\mathsf{augment}_{T'}$ obeying the following rules:

- typing rule:
$$
\frac{(C, \Theta) \in U_{T'A}\text{-}\mathbf{cone} \quad f : A \to TB}{\mathsf{augment}_{T',C}(\Theta, f) : C \to TB}
$$

- β-conversion rule (= FOLD/AUGMENT fusion law):
$$
\frac{(C, \Theta) \in U_{T'A}\text{-}\mathbf{cone} \quad f : A \to TB \quad (X, \varphi) \in T'B\text{-}\mathbf{alg}}{\mathsf{fold}_{T'B,X}\, \varphi \circ \mathsf{augment}_{T',C}(\Theta, f) = \Theta_X\,(\varphi \circ (T'B\,(\mathsf{fold}_{T'B,X}\, \varphi) \circ \alpha_B^{-1} \circ f)^\circ)}
$$

- conversion rules relating to the monad structure:
$$
\frac{(C, \Theta) \in U_{T'A}\text{-}\mathbf{cone} \quad f : A \to TB}{\mathsf{augment}_{T',C}(\Theta, f) = f^\star \circ \mathsf{build}_{T'A,C}\Theta} \qquad \frac{(C, \Theta) \in U_{T'A}\text{-}\mathbf{cone}}{\mathsf{build}_{T'A,C}\Theta = \mathsf{augment}_{T',C}(\Theta, \eta_A)}
$$

$$
\frac{(C, \Theta) \in U_{T'A}\text{-}\mathbf{cone} \quad f : A \to TB \quad g : B \to TC}{g^\star \circ \mathsf{augment}_{T',C}(\Theta, f) = \mathsf{augment}_{T',C}(\Theta, g^\star \circ f)}
$$

Notice that the first two rules in the last group state that the AUGMENT and BUILD combinators are interdefinable using the unit and bind of the monad.

Instantiating the first of them with $(C, \Theta) = (TA, \text{fold}_{T'A})$, we obtain that bind is AUGMENT applied to FOLD:

$$\frac{f : A \rightarrow TB}{\text{augment}_{T', TA}(\text{fold}_{T'A}, f) = f^{\star}}$$

Combining this with the FOLD/AUGMENT fusion rule, we get the following rule for fusing FOLD with bind:

$$\frac{f : A \rightarrow TB \quad (X, \varphi) \in T'B\text{-}\mathbf{alg}}{\text{fold}_{T'B, X}\varphi \circ f^{\star} = \text{fold}_{T'A, X}(\varphi \circ (T'B(\text{fold}_{T'B, X}\varphi) \circ \alpha_B^{-1} \circ f)^{\circ})}$$

Here is an implementation of finitely branching node labelled trees (rose trees) in Haskell, including the monad structure.

```
data Tree a = Node a [Tree a]

foldT :: (a -> [x] -> x) -> Tree a -> x
foldT phi (Node a tas) = phi a (map (foldT phi) tas)

instance Monad Tree where
  return a = Node a []
  ta >>= f = foldT (\ a tbs' -> let Node b tbs = f a
                                in Node b (tbs ++ tbs')) ta
```

The BUILD and AUGMENT combinators are implementable as follows:

```
buildT :: (forall x . (a -> [x] -> x) -> x) -> Tree a
buildT theta = theta Node

augmentT :: (forall x . (a -> [x] -> x) -> x)
                        -> (a -> Tree b) -> Tree b
augmentT theta f = theta (\ a tbs' -> let Node b tbs = f a
                                      in Node b (tbs ++ tbs'))
```

FOLD/BUILD fusion and FOLD/AUGMENT fusion say that

```
foldT phi (buildT theta) == theta phi
foldT phi (augmentT theta f) == theta (\ a xs ->
                        let Node b tbs = f a
                        in phi b (map (foldT phi) tbs ++ xs))
```

For inductive hyperfunction spaces, we get the BUILD and AUGMENT combinators as follows:

```
data Hyper e a = H { unH :: (Hyper e a -> e) -> a }
```

```
foldH :: (((x -> e) -> a) -> x) -> Hyper e a -> x
foldH phi (H h) = phi (\ g -> h (g . foldH phi))

instance Monad (Hyper e) where
  return a = H (const a)
  ha >>= f = foldH (\ g -> H (\ k -> unH (f (g k)) k)) ha

buildH :: (forall x . (((x -> e) -> a) -> x) -> x)
                                               -> Hyper e a
buildH theta = theta H

augmentH :: (forall x . (((x -> e) -> a) -> x) -> x)
                             -> (a -> Hyper e b) -> Hyper e b
augmentH theta f = theta (\ g -> H (\ k -> unH (f (g k)) k))
```

The corresponding fusion laws are

```
foldH phi (buildH theta) == theta phi
foldH phi (augmentH theta f) ==
    theta (\ g -> phi (\ k -> unH (f (g k)) (k . foldH phi)))
```

Finally, the general construction of monads from parameterized monads via initial algebras may also be implemented generically:

```
class Monad' m where
  return' :: a -> m a x
  (>>|) :: m a x -> (a -> m b x) -> m b x
  fmap' :: (x -> y) -> (m a x -> m a y)

data Mu m a = In {unIn :: m a (Mu m a) }

fold :: Monad' m  => (m a x -> x) -> Mu m a -> x
fold phi (In tas) = phi (fmap' (fold phi) tas)

instance Monad' m => Monad (Mu m) where
  return a = In (return' a)
  ta >>= f = fold (In . (>>| unIn . f)) ta

build :: (forall x. (m a x -> x) -> x) -> Mu m a
build theta = theta In

augment :: Monad' m => (forall x. (m a x -> x) -> x)
                             -> (a -> Mu m b) -> Mu m b
augment theta f = theta (In . (>>| unIn . f))
```

The corresponding FOLD/BUILD and FOLD/AUGMENT fusion rules are as follows:

```
fold phi (build theta) == theta phi
fold phi (augment theta f) ==
    theta (phi . (>>| fmap' (fold phi) . unIn . f))
```

5.5 CONCLUSION AND FUTURE WORK

We have demonstrated that the semantics of inductive types in terms of limits of algebra structure forgetting functors does not only explain the typing (including, notably, the coherence condition on the argument) of the BUILD combinator and the FOLD/BUILD fusion rule, but exhibits a flexibility thanks to which it is not hard to generalize Gill's originally rather specific AUGMENT combinator to a considerably wider class of parameterized inductive types. This reveals, in particular, that the original FOLD/AUGMENT fusion for lists, which at first sight looks like an ad hoc rule, is really a special case of a very systematic rule, a tip of a small iceberg.

As future work we plan to achieve a similar account for the vanish combinators of Voigtländer [Voi02]. We also plan to study the relation of strong dinaturality and parametricity.

Acknowledgments. The authors were partially supported by the Royal Society ESEP programme within joint research project No. 15642. The second and third author were also partially supported by the Estonian Science Foundation under grant No. 5567.

REFERENCES

[GUV04] N. Ghani, T. Uustalu, and V. Vene. Build, augment and destroy, universally. In W.-N. Chin, *Proc. of 2nd Asian Symp. on Programming Languages and Systems, APLAS'04*, v. 3302 of *Lect. Notes in Comput. Sci.*, pp. 327–347. Springer-Verlag, Berlin, 2004.

[GLP93] A. Gill, J. Launchbury, and S. L. Peyton Jones. A short cut to deforestation. In *Conf. Record of 6th ACM SIGPLAN-SIGARCH Int. Conf. on Functional Programming Languages and Computer Architecture, FPCA'93*, pp. 223–232. ACM Press, 1993.

[Gil96] A. J. Gill. *Cheap Deforestation for Non-strict Functional Languages*. PhD thesis, Univ. of Glasgow, 1996.

[Hag87] T. Hagino. A typed lambda calculus with categorical type constructors. In D. H. Pitt, A. Poign, and D. E. Rydeheard, eds., *Proc. of 2nd Int. Conf. on Category Theory and Computer Science, CTCS'87*, v. 283 of *Lecture Notes in Computer Science*, pp. 140–157. Springer-Verlag, Berlin, 1987.

[Joh02] P. Johann. A generalization of short-cut fusion and its correctness proof. *Higher-Order and Symbolic Computation*, 15(4):273–300, 2002.

[Joh03] P. Johann. Short-cut fusion is correct. *J. of Functional Programming*, 13(4):797–814, 2003.

[KLP01] S. Krstiæ, J. Launchbury, and D. Pavloviæ. Categories of processes enriched in final coalgebras. In F. Honsell and M. Miculan, eds., *Proc. of 4th Int. Conf. on Found. of Software Science and Computation Structures, FoSSaCS'01*, v. 2030 of *Lect. Notes in Comput. Sci.*, pp. 303–317. Springer-Verlag, Berlin, 2001.

[LS95]   J. Launchbury and T. Sheard. Warm fusion: Deriving build-catas from recursive
          definitions. In *Conf. Record 7th ACM SIGPLAN-SIGARCH Int. Conf. on Func-
          tional Programming Languages and Computer Architecture, FPCA'95*, pp. 314–
          323. ACM Press, 1995.

[TM95]   A. Takano and E. Meijer. Shortcut deforestation in calculational form. In *Conf.
          Record 7th of ACM SIGPLAN/SIGARCH Int. Conf. on Functional Programming
          Languages and Computer Architecture, FPCA'95*, pp. 306–313. ACM Press,
          1995.

[Uus03]   T. Uustalu. Generalizing substitution. *Theoretical Informatics and Applications*,
          37(4):315-336, 2003.

[Voi02]   J. Voigtländer. Concatenate, reverse and map vanish for free. In *Proc. of 7th
          ACM SIGPLAN Int. Conf. on Functional Programming, ICFP'02*, v. 37(9) of
          SIGPLAN Notices, pp. 14–25. ACM Press, 2002.

[Wad89]   P. Wadler. Theorems for free! In *Proc. of 4th Int. Conf. on Funct. Prog. Lan-
          guages and Computer Arch., FPCA'89*, pp. 347–359. ACM Press, 1989.

Chapter 6

Alice Through the Looking Glass

Andreas Rossberg[1], Didier Le Botlan[1], Guido Tack[1], Thorsten Brunklaus[1], Gert Smolka[1]

Abstract: We present Alice, a functional programming language that has been designed with strong support for *typed open programming*. It incorporates concurrency with data flow synchronisation, higher-order modularity, dynamic modules, and type-safe pickling as a minimal and generic set of simple, orthogonal features providing that support. Based on these mechanisms Alice offers a flexible notion of component, and high-level facilities for distributed programming.

6.1   INTRODUCTION

Software is decreasingly delivered as a closed, monolithic whole. As its complexity and the need for integration grows it becomes more and more important to allow flexible dynamic acquisition of additional functionality. Program execution is no longer restricted to one local machine only: with net-oriented applications being omni-present, programs are increasingly distributed across local or global networks. As a result, programs need to exchange more data with more structure. In particular, they need to exchange behaviour, that is, data may include code.

We refer to development for the described scenario as *open programming*. Our understanding of open programming includes the following main characteristics:

- *Modularity*, to flexibly combine software blocks that were created separately.
- *Dynamicity*, to import *and* export software blocks in running programs.
- *Security*, to safely deal with unknown or untrusted software blocks.
- *Distribution*, to communicate data and software blocks over networks.
- *Concurrency*, to deal with asynchronous events and non-sequential tasks.

---

[1]Programming Systems Lab, Saarland University, Saarbrücken, Germany;
E-mail: rossberg,botlan,tack,brunklaus,smolka@ps.uni-sb.de

Dynamic software blocks are usually called *components*.

Most practical programming languages today have not been designed with open programming in mind. Even the few that have been – primarily Java [GJS96] – do not adequately address all of the above points. For example, Java is not statically type-safe, has only weak support for import/export, and rather clunky distribution and concurrency mechanisms.

Our claim is that only a few simple, orthogonal concepts are necessary to provide a flexible, *strongly typed* framework supporting all aspects of open programming. Components are a central notion in this framework, but instead of being primitive they can be derived from the following simpler, orthogonal concepts:

- *Futures*, which allow for light-weight concurrency and *laziness*.
- *Higher-order modules*, to provide genericity and encapsulation.
- *Packages*, to wrap modules into self-describing, dynamically typed entities.
- *Pickling*, to enable generic persistence and distribution.
- *Proxy functions*, to enable remote calls into other processes.

To substantiate our claim, we developed the programming language *Alice ML*, a conservative extension of Standard ML [MTHM97]. It is largely inspired by Oz [Smo95, Moz04, VH04], a relational language with advanced support for open programming, but lacking any notion of static typing. The aim of the Alice project is to systematically reconstruct the essential functionality of Oz on top of a typed functional language.

Alice has been implemented in the Alice Programming System [Ali04], a full-featured programming environment based on a VM with just-in-time compilation, support for platform-independent persistence and platform-independent mobile code, and a rich library for constraint programming.

Organisation of the paper.   This paper describes the design of the open programming features of Alice. Futures provide for concurrency (Section 6.2). Higher-order modules enhance modularity (Section 6.3). Type-safe marshalling is enabled by packages (Section 6.4). Components (Section 6.5) are built on top of these mechanism (Section 6.6). Distribution is based on components and RPCs (Section 6.7). We briefly discuss the implementation (Section 6.8), compare to some related work (Section 6.9), and conclude with a short outlook (Section 6.10).

6.2 FUTURES

Programs communicating with the outside world usually have to deal with non-deterministic, asynchronous events. Purely sequential programming cannot adequately handle such scenarios. Support for concurrency hence is vital.

Concurrency in Alice is based uniformly on the concept of *futures*, which has been mostly adapted from Multilisp [Hal85]. A future is a transparent placeholder for a yet undetermined value that allows for implicit synchronisation based on data flow. There are different kinds of futures, which we will describe in the following sections. A formal semantics can be found in [NSS02]. Futures are a generic mechanism for communication and synchronisation. As such, they are comparatively simple, but expressive enough to enable formulation of a broad range of concurrency abstractions.

6.2.1 Concurrency

Future-based concurrency is very light-weight: any expression can be evaluated in its own thread, a simple keyword allows forking off a concurrent computation:

spawn *exp*

This phrase immediately evaluates to a fresh *concurrent future*, standing for the yet unknown result of *exp*. Simultaneously, evaluation of *exp* is initiated in a new thread. As soon as the thread terminates, the result globally replaces the future.

A thread is said to *touch* a future [FF95] when it performs an operation that requires the actual value the future stands for. A thread that touches a future is suspended automatically until the actual value is determined. This is known as *data flow synchronisation*.

If a concurrent thread terminates with an exception, the respective future is said to be *failed*. Any operation touching a failed future will cause the respective exception to be synchronously re-raised in the current thread.

Thanks to futures, threads give results, and concurrency can be orthogonally introduced for arbitrary parts of an expression. We hence speak of *functional threads*. For example, to evaluate all constituents of the application $e_1(e_2,e_3)$ concurrently, it is sufficient to annotate the application as follows:

(**spawn** e_1) (**spawn** e_2, **spawn** e_3)

Functional threads allow turning a synchronous function call to a function f into an *asynchronous* one by simply prefixing the application with spawn:

val result = **spawn** f (x, y, z)

The ease of making asynchronous calls even where a result is required is important in combination with distributed programming (Section 6.7), because it allows for *lag tolerance*: the caller can continue its computation while waiting for the result to be delivered. Data flow synchronisation ensures that it will wait if necessary, but at the latest possible time, thus maximising concurrency.

Futures already provide for complex communication and synchronisation. Consider the following example:

val offset = **spawn** (sleep(Time.fromSeconds 120); 20)
val table = Vector.tabulate (40, **fn** i ⇒ **spawn** fib(i + offset))

The first declaration starts a thread that takes two minutes to deliver the value 20. The computation for the table entries in the second declaration depends on that value, but since the entries are computed concurrently, construction of the table can proceed without delay. However, the spawned threads will all block until offset is determined. Consecutive code can already access the table, but if it touches an entry that is not yet determined, it will automatically block.

Besides implicit synchronisation, Alice offers primitives for explicit synchronisation, including non-deterministic choice. They are sufficient to encode complex synchronisation with multiple events or timeouts [RLT+04].

6.2.2 Laziness

It has become a common desire to marry eager and lazy evaluation, and the future
mechanism provides an elegant way to do so. While keeping eager application
semantics, full support for laziness is available through *lazy futures*: the phrase

    lazy *exp*

will not evaluate *exp*, but instead returns a fresh lazy future, standing for the yet
unknown result of *exp*. Evaluation of *exp* is triggered by a thread first touching the future. At that moment, the lazy future becomes a concurrent future and
evaluation proceeds as for concurrent futures.

In other words, lazy evaluation can be selected for individual expressions. For
example, the expression (fn x $\Rightarrow$ 5) (lazy raise E) will *not* raise E. A fully lazy
evaluation regime can be emulated by prefixing *every* subexpression with lazy.

6.2.3 Promises and locking

Functional threads and lazy evaluation offer convenient means to introduce and
eliminate futures. However, the direct coupling between a future and the computation delivering its value often is too inflexible. *Promises* are a more fine-grained
mechanism that allows for creation and elimination of futures in separate operations, based on three basic primitives:

    type α promise
    val promise : unit $\rightarrow \alpha$ promise
    val future : α promise $\rightarrow \alpha$
    val fulfill : α promise $\times \alpha \rightarrow$ unit

A promise is an explicit handle for a future. Creating one by calling promise vir-
tually states the assurance that a suitable value determining that *promised future*
will be made available at some later point in time, fulfilling the promise. The future itself is obtained by applying the future function to the promise. A promised
future is not replaced automatically, but has to be eliminated by explicitly applying the fulfill function to its promise. A promise may only be fulfilled once, any
further attempt will raise the exception Promise.

Promises allow for partial and top-down construction of data structures with
holes, e.g. a tail-recursive formulation of the append function [RLT+04]. However, they are particularly important for concurrent programming: for example,
they can be used to implement streams and channels as lists with a promised tail.
They also provide an important primitive for programming synchronisation.

For instance, Alice requires no primitive locking mechanisms, they can be
fully bootstrapped from promises plus atomic exchange on references, a variant
of the fundamental test-and-set operation [Hal85]:

```
(* mutex : unit → (α → β) → (α → β) *)
fun mutex () = let
      val r = ref ()                              (* create lock *)
   in
      fn f ⇒ fn x ⇒ let
            val p = promise ()
         in
            await (exchange (r, future p));   (* take lock *)
            f x
            finally fulfill (p, ())              (* release lock *)
         end
   end
end
```

FIGURE 6.1.   Mutexes for synchronised functions

---

val exchange : α ref × α → α

As a demonstrating example, Figure 6.1 presents a function implementing mutex locks for synchronising an arbitrary number of argument functions.[2] The following snippet illustrates its use to ensure non-interleaved concurrent output:

```
val sync = mutex ()
val f = sync (fn x ⇒ (print "x = "; print x; print "\n"))
val g = sync (fn y ⇒ (print y; print "\n"))
spawn f "A"; spawn g "B"
```

6.2.4   Modules and types

Futures are not restricted to the core language, entire modules can be futures, too: module expressions can be evaluated lazily or concurrently by explicitly prefixing them with the corresponding keywords lazy or spawn. In Section 6.5 we will see that lazy module futures are ubiquitous as a consequence of the lazy linking mechanism for components.

The combination of module futures and dynamic types (Section 6.4) also implies the existence of *type futures*. They are touched only by the unpack operation (Section 6.4.1) and by pickling (Section 6.4.2). Touching a type generally can trigger arbitrary computations, e.g. by loading a component (Section 6.5).

6.3   HIGHER-ORDER MODULES

For open programming, good language support for modularity is essential. The SML module system is quite advanced, but still limited. Adopting a long line of work [DCH03, Ler95, Lil97, Rus98], Alice extends it with higher-order functors and local modules (for dealing with packages, Section 6.4).

---

[2] Alice defines *exp*$_1$ finally *exp*$_2$ as syntactic sugar for executing a finaliser *exp*$_2$ after evaluation of *exp*$_1$ regardless of any exceptional termination.

Less standard is the support for nested and abstract signatures: as in Objective Caml, signatures can be put into structures and even be specified abstractly in other signatures. Abstract signatures have received little attention previously, but they are interesting because they enable the definition of *polymorphic functors*, exemplified by a generic application functor:

functor Apply (**signature** S **signature** T) (F: S → T) (X: S) = F X

Polymorphic functors are used in the Alice library to provide certain functionality at the module level (see e.g. Section 6.7.3). More importantly, nested signatures turn structures into a general container for all language entities, which is crucial for the design of the component system (Section 6.5). The presence of abstract signatures renders module type checking undecidable [Lil97], but this has not turned out to be a problem in practice.

6.4 PACKAGES

When a program is able to import and export functionality dynamically, from statically unknown sources, a certain amount of runtime checking is inevitable to ensure the integrity of the program and the runtime system. In particular, it must be ensured that dynamic imports cannot undermine the type system.

Dynamics [Myc83, ACPR95] complement static typing with isolated dynamic type checking. They provide a universal type dyn of 'dynamic values' that carry runtime type information. Values of every type can be injected, projection is a complex type-case operation that dispatches on the runtime type found in the dynamic value. Dynamics adequately solve the problem of typed open programming by demanding external values to uniformly have type dyn. We see several hurdles that nevertheless prevented the wide-spread adoption of dynamics in practice: (1) their too fine level of granularity, (2) the complexity of the type-case construct, (3) the lack of flexibility with matching types.

We modified the concept of dynamics slightly: dynamics in Alice, called *packages*, contain *modules*. Projection simply matches the runtime *package signature* against a static one – with full respect for subtyping. Reusing module subtyping has several advantages: (1) it keeps the language simple, (2) it is flexible and sufficiently robust against interface evolution, and (3) it allows the programmer to naturally adopt idioms already known from modular programming. Moreover, packages allow modules to be passed as first-class values, a capability that is sometimes being missed from ML, and becomes increasingly important with open programming. A formal semantics for packages can be found in [Ros05].

6.4.1 Basics

A package is a value of the abstract type package. Intuitively, it contains a module, along with a dynamic description of its signature. A package is created by injecting a module, expressed by a structure expressions *strexp* in SML:[3]

---
[3]Since Alice supports higher-order modules, *strexp* includes functor expressions.

pack *strexp* : *sigexp*

The signature expression *sigexp* defines the package signature. The inverse operation is projection, eliminating a package. The module expression

unpack *exp* : *sigexp*

takes a package computed by *exp* and extracts the contained module, provided that the package signature matches the *target signature* denoted by *sigexp*. Statically, the expression has the signature *sigexp*. If the dynamic check fails, the pre-defined exception Unpack is raised.

A package can be understood as a statically typed first-class module as proposed by Russo [Rus00, Rus98], wrapped into a conventional dynamic. However, coupling both mechanisms enables unpack to exploit subtype polymorphism, which is not possible otherwise, due to the lack of subtyping in the ML core language.

6.4.2 Pickling

The primary purpose of packages is to type dynamic import and export of high-level language objects. At the core of this functionality lies a service called *pickling*. Pickling takes a value and produces a transitively closed, platform-independent representation of it, such that an equivalent copy can be constructed in other processes. Since ML is a language with first-class functions, a pickle can naturally include code. Thanks to packages, even entire modules can be pickled.

One obvious application of pickling is *persistence*, available through two primitives in the library structure Pickle:

val save : string × package → unit
val load : string → package

The save operation writes a package to a file of a given name. Any future occurring in the package (including lazy ones) will be touched (Section 6.2.1). If the package contains a local *resource*, i.e. a value that is private to a process, then the exception Sited is raised (we return to the issue of resources in Section 6.5.3). The inverse operation load retrieves a package from a file.

For example, we can write the library structure Array to disk:

Pickle.save ("array.alc", **pack** Array : ARRAY)

It can be retrieved again with the inverse sequence of operations:

structure Array1 = **unpack** Pickle.load "array.alc" : ARRAY

Any attempt to unpack it with an incompatible signature will fail with an Unpack exception. All subsequent accesses to Array1 or members of it are statically type-safe, the only possible point of type failure is the unpack operation.

Note that the type Array1.array will be statically incompatible with the original type Array.array, since there is no way to know statically what type identities are found in a package, and all types in the target signature must hence be considered abstract. If compatibility is required, it can be enforced in the usual ML way, namely by putting *sharing constraints* on the target signature:

```
structure Array1 = unpack Pickle.load "/tmp/array.alc"
                       : ARRAY where type array = Array.array
```

6.4.3 Parametricity, abstraction safety and generativity

By utilising dynamic type sharing it is possible to dynamically test for type equiv-
alences. In other words, evaluation is no longer *parametric* [Rey83]. For example,

```
functor F (type t) = unpack load file : (val it : t)
```

is a functor that behaves differently depending on what type t it is passed.[4]

Parametricity is important because it induces strong static invariants about
polymorphic types, that particularly guarantee *abstraction* [Rey83] and enable
efficient type erasing compilation. On the other hand, packages enforce the presence of non-parametric behaviour. Alice thus has been designed such that the *core*
language, where polymorphism is ubiquitous, maintains parametricity. Only the
module level employs dynamic type information – module evaluation can be type-
dependent. This design reduces the costs for dynamic types and provides a clear
model for the programmer: only *explicit* types can affect the dynamic semantics.

The absence of parametricity on the module level still raises the question of
how dynamic typing interferes with type abstraction. Can we sneak through an
abstraction barrier by dynamically discovering an abstract type's representation?
For instance:

```
signature S = (type t; val x : t)
structure M = (type t = int; val x = 37) :> S
structure N = unpack (pack M : S) : (S where type t = int)
val y = N.x + 1
```

Fortunately, the unpack operation will fail at runtime, due to a *dynamically gen-
erative* interpretation of type abstraction: with every abstraction operator :> evaluated, fresh type names are generated dynamically [Ros03]. Abstraction safety is
always maintained, even when whole modules cross process boundaries, because
type names are globally unique.

Note that when fully dynamic type generativity is too strong to achieve proper
type sharing between processes, the implementation of an abstract type can simply
be exported as a pre-evaluated component (Section 6.5.4).

6.5 COMPONENTS

Software of non-trivial complexity has to be split into functional building blocks
that can be created separately and configured dynamically. Such blocks are called
components. We distinguish components from modules: while modules provide
name spacing, genericity, and encapsulation, components provide physical separation and dynamic composition. Both mechanisms complement each other.

---

[4]Alice allows abbreviating signatures sig ... end with (...), likewise for structures.

Alice incorporates a powerful notion of component that is a refinement and extension of the component system found in the Oz language [DKSS98], which in turn was partially inspired by Java [GJS96]. It provides all of the following:

- *Separate compilation*. Components are physically separate program units.
- *Lazy dynamic linking*. Loading is performed automatically when needed.
- *Static linking*. Components can be bundled into larger components off-line.
- *Dynamic creation*. Components can be computed and exported at runtime.
- *Type safety*. Components carry type information and linking checks it.
- *Flexibility*. Type checking is tolerant against interface changes.
- *Sandboxing*. Custom *component managers* enable selective import policies.

6.5.1 Introduction

A program consists of a – potentially open – set of components that are created separately and loaded dynamically. Static linking allows both to be performed on a different level of granularity by bundling given components to form larger ones. Every component defines a module – its *export*, and accesses an arbitrary number of modules from other components – its *imports*. Import and export interfaces are fully typed by ML signatures.

Each Alice source file defines a component. Syntactically, it is a sequence of SML declarations that is interpreted as a structure body, forming the export module. The respective export signature is inferred by the compiler. A component can access other components through a prologue of import declarations:

import *spec* **from** *string*

The SML signature specification *spec* in an import declaration describes the entities used from the imported structure, along with their type. Because of Alice's higher-order modules (Section 6.3), these entities can include functors and even signatures. The string contains the URL under which the component is to be acquired at runtime. The exact interpretation of the URL is up to the component manager (Section 6.5.3), but usually it is either a local file, an HTTP web address, or a virtual URL denoting local library components. For instance:

import structure Server : **sig val** run : $(\alpha{\to}\beta) \to (\alpha{\to}\beta)$ **end**
  from "http://domain.org/server"

For convenience, Alice allows the type annotations in import specifications to be dropped. In that case, the imported component must be accessible (in compiled form) during compilation, so that the compiler can insert the respective types.

6.5.2 Program execution and dynamic linking

A designated *root* is the main component of a program. To execute a program, its root component is evaluated. Loading of imported components is performed *lazily*, and every component is loaded and evaluated only once. This is achieved

by treating every cross-component reference as a lazy future (Section 6.2.2). The
process of loading a component requested as import by another one is referred to
as *dynamic linking*. It involves several steps:

- *Resolution*. The import URL is normalised to a canonical form.
- *Acquisition*. If the component is being requested for the first time, it is loaded.
- *Evaluation*. If the component has been loaded afresh, its body is evaluated.
- *Type Checking*. The component's export signature is matched against the re-
  spective import signature.

Each of the steps can fail: the component might be inaccessible or malformed,
evaluation may terminate with an exception, or type checking may discover a
mismatch. Under each of these circumstances, the respective future is failed with
a standard exception that carries a description of the precise cause of the failure.

6.5.3   Component managers and sandboxing

Linking is performed with the help of a *component manager*, which is a module
of the runtime library, similar to a class loader in Java [GJS96]. It is responsible
for locating and loading components, and keeping a table of loaded components.

In an open setting it is important to be able to deal with untrusted components.
For example, they should not be given write access to the local file system. Like
Java, Alice can execute components in a *sandbox*. Sandboxing relies on two factors: (1) all resources and capabilities a component needs for execution are *sited*
and have to be acquired via import through a component manager (in particular,
they cannot be stored in a pickle); (2) it is possible to create custom managers and
link components through them. A custom manager can never grant more access
than it has itself. A custom manager hence represents a proper sandbox.

6.5.4   Dynamic creation of components

The external representation of a component is a pickle. It is hence possible to
create a component not only statically by compilation, but also dynamically, by
a running Alice program. In fact, a pickle created with the Pickle.save function
(Section 6.4.2) *is* a component and can be imported as such.

The ability to create components dynamically is particularly important for distribution (Section 6.7.3). Basically, it enables components to capture dynamically
obtained information, e.g. configuration data or connections to other processes.

6.6   DECOMPOSING COMPONENTS

What *are* components? The close relation to concepts presented in previous chap-
ters, like modules, packages and futures is obvious, so one might hope that there
exists a simple reduction from components to simpler concepts. And indeed, components are merely syntactic sugar. Basically, a component defined by a sequence
of declarations *dec* is interpreted as a higher-order procedure:

> **fn** *link* ⇒ **pack struct** *dec* **end** : *sigexp*

where *link* is a reserved identifier and *sigexp* is the component signature derived by the compiler (the principal signature). In *dec*, every import declaration

> **import** *spec* **from** *s*

is rewritten as[5]

> **structure** *strid* = **lazy unpack** *link s* : **sig** *spec* **end**
> **open** *strid*

where *strid* is a fresh identifier. The expansion makes laziness and dynamic type checking of imports immediately obvious. Component acquisition is encapsulated in the component manager represented by the *link* procedure. Every component receives that procedure for acquiring its imports and evaluates to a package that contains its own export. The *link* procedure has type string → package, taking a URL and returning a package representing the export of the respective component. Imports are structure declarations that lazily unpack that package.

When a component is requested for the first time the *link* procedure loads it, evaluates it and enters it into a table. Figure 6.2 contains a simple model implementation that assumes existence of two auxiliary procedures *resolve*, for normalising URLs relative to the URL of the parent component, and *acquire* for loading a component. The parent URL is required as an additional parameter to enable the respective resolution. To achieve proper re-entrancy, the manager uses promises to implement locking on the component table (Section 6.2.3), and unlocks it *before* evaluating the component (hence the lazy application).

Giving this reduction of components, execution of an Alice program can be thought of as evaluation of the simple application

> link "." root

where link is the initial component manager and *root* is the URL of the program's root component, resolved relative to the 'current' location, which we indicate by a dot here.

6.7 DISTRIBUTION

Distributed programming can be based on only a few high-level primitives that suffice to hide all the embarrassing details of low-level communication.

6.7.1 Proxies

The central concept for distribution in Alice are *proxies*. A proxy is a mobile wrapper for a stationary function: it can be pickled and transferred to other processes without transferring the wrapped function itself. When a proxy function is applied, the call is automatically forwarded to the original site as a remote invocation, where argument and result are automatically transferred by means of pickling.

---

[5]An open declaration merely affects scoping, it does not touch its argument.

```
val table = ref [] : (url × package) list ref

fun link parent url = let
    val url' = resolve (parent, url)              (* get absolute URL *)
    val p = promise ()
    val table' = exchange (table, future p)       (* lock table *)
in
    case List.find (fn (x,y) ⇒ x = url') table' of
        SOME package ⇒                            (* already loaded *)
            (fulfill (p, table'); package)        (* unlock, return *)
      | NONE ⇒ let                                (* not loaded yet *)
            val component = acquire url'           (* load component *)
            val package = lazy component(link url')             (* evaluate *)

        in
            fulfill (p, (url',package) :: table');  (* unlock *)
            package
        end
end
```

FIGURE 6.2.   The essence of a component manager

Proxies are created using the primitive

val proxy : $(\alpha \rightarrow \beta) \rightarrow (\alpha \rightarrow \beta)$

For instance, the expression proxy (**fn** x ⇒ x+1) creates a simple proxy.

All invocations of a proxy are synchronous. In order to make an asynchronous call, it suffices to wrap the application using spawn (Section 6.2.1). This immediately returns a future that will be replaced by the result of the remote call automatically once it terminates.

Note that all calls through proxies are statically typed.

6.7.2   Client/server

To initiate a proxy connection, a pickle must be first transferred between processes by other means. The Alice library supports two main scenarios. In the *client/server* model a client establishes a connection to a known server. A service offered by a server takes the form of a local component, which we refer to as the *mobile* component. Mobile components can be made available in a network through a simple transfer mechanism adapted from Mozart [Moz04]. To employ it, a component is first packaged (Section 6.4), and then made available for download:

val offer : package → url

Given a package (Section 6.4), this function returns a URL, called a *ticket*, which publicly identifies the package in the network. A ticket can be communicated to the outside world by conventional means such as web pages, e-mail, phone, or pigeons. A client can use a ticket to retrieve the package from the server:

val take : url → package

The package can then be opened using unpack, which dynamically checks that the package signature matches the client's expectations. Noticeably, this is the only point where a dynamic type check is necessary.

In order to establish a permanent connection, the mobile component must contain proxies. More complex communication patterns can be established by passing proxies back and forth via other proxies. They can even be forwarded to third parties, for instance to enable different clients to communicate directly.

6.7.3   Master/slave

In an alternative scenario a *master* initiates shifting computational tasks to a number of *slave* computers. The library functor Run performs most of the respective procedure: it connects to a remote machine by using a low-level service (such as ssh), and starts a slave process that immediately connects to the master. It evaluates a component and sends back the result.

```
functor Run (val host : string
              signature RESULT
              functor F : COMPONENT·MANAGER → RESULT) : RESULT
```

Run is a polymorphic functor (Section 6.3) with two concrete arguments: the name of the remote host, and a functor that basically defines a dynamic component (Section 6.5.4). It takes a structure representing a component manager, which can be used to access local libraries and resources on the remote host.

We illustrate a two-way connection by sketching the implementation of a distributed computation. A master process delegates computations to slaves that may dynamically request data from the master, by calling the proxy getData. For simplicity, we assume that the result of the computation is an integer.

```
(* Slaves use getData to acquire specific data. *)
val getData = proxy (fn key ⇒ return associated data)

(* Create a slave process on the given host. *)
fun computeOn (hostname, parameter) = let
    functor Start (CM : COMPONENT·MANAGER) = (val result = computa-
tion)
    structure Slave = Run (val host = hostname
                            signature RESULT = (val result : int)
                            functor F = Start)
in
    Slave.result
end
```

In the definition of result, the computation may use getData, which is a proxy to the master. It can access local libraries through the component manager CM. Note also that the computation is parameterised by the argument parameter. Then, the following code suffices to perform distributed computations in parallel.

```
val res1 = spawn computeOn ("machine1", parameter1)
val res2 = spawn computeOn ("machine2", parameter2)
```

The extended version of this paper contains a more extensive example [RLT$^+$04].

6.8   IMPLEMENTATION

An implementation of Alice must meet two key requirements: dealing efficiently with the future-based concurrency model, and supporting open programming by providing a truly platform-independent and generic pickling mechanism.

The appropriate technology to achieve platform independence is to use a virtual machine (VM) together with just-in-time (JIT) compilation to native machine code. Futures and light-weight threads are implemented at the core of the system, making concurrency and data flow synchronisation efficient.

Pickling and unpickling are core VM services and available for all data in the store. They preserve cycles and sharing, which is vital for efficient pickling. Alice also features a minimisation mechanism that merges all equivalent subgraphs of a pickled data graph [Tac03].

Code is just heap-allocated data, it is subject to garbage collection and can be pickled and unpickled. The VM allows different internal types of code – e.g. JIT compiled native code and interpreted byte code – to coexist and cooperate. Different codes and interpreters can be selected on a per-procedure basis. Pickler and unpickler automatically convert between these internal codes and a well-defined external format. More details can be found in [RLT$^+$04] and in a technical report [BK02].

Thanks to the pickling-based approach to distribution no complex distributed garbage collection is required. The only inter-process references are proxies. Distributed collection of proxies will be implemented in a future version of Alice.

6.9   RELATED WORK

There is numerous work and languages concerned with some of the issues addressed by Alice. A more detailed and extensive comparison can be found in [RLT$^+$04].

Java [GJS96] was the first major language designed for open programming. It is object-oriented and open programming is based on *reflection*, which allows other components to exploit type information constructively. We feel that general reflection is expensive, invites abuse, and in practice demands a rather limited type system, while packages avoid these issues. Concurrency and serialisation require considerable support from the programmer, code cannot be serialised. No structural type checks are performed when a class is loaded, subsequent method calls may cause a NoSuchMethodError, undermining the type system.

Scala [Ode05] is a hybrid object-oriented/functional language on top of the Java infrastructure. It has a very powerful static type system with expressive abstraction mechanisms. For example, *bounded views* can specify a lower bound as well as an upper bound for an abstracted type. For comparison, a signature in Alice is a lower bound of the abstracted component. Still, concurrency and distribution are inherited from Java and suffer from the same shortcomings. In particular, the expressiveness of the type system does not carry over to dynamic typing, because Scala types are *erased* to Java types during compilation.

Oz/Mozart [Smo95, Moz04, VH04] inspired many of the concepts in Alice. Oz has very similar high-level support for concurrency, pickling and components. The Mozart distribution subsystem is more ambitious than Alice, supporting distributed state and futures, for the price of considerably higher complexity. Unlike Alice, Oz is based on a relational core language. It has no type system.

Acute [SLW+04] is probably closest in spirit to Alice. It is an experimental ML-based language for typed open programming that guarantees safe interaction between distributed applications, although the details of distribution are left to the programmer. Pickling allows resources to be dynamically rebound, no respective safety mechanism is built in. Components support versioning, but look more ad-hoc compared to Alice. Unlike in Alice, abstractions can be broken by explicit means, for the sake of flexible versioning.

JoCaml [FMS01] is an innovative distributed extension of OCaml based on the Join calculus. Concurrency and distribution uses channels and is more high-level than in Alice, allowing for complex declarative synchronisation patterns and thread migration. However, JoCaml is not open: pickling is restricted to monomorphic values stored on a global name server and there is no explicit component concept.

CML [Rep99] is a mature concurrent extension of SML. It is based on first-class channels and synchronisation events, where synchronization has to be fully explicit. CML does not address distribution or other aspects of open programming.

Erlang [AVWW96] is a language designed for embedded distributed applications, applied successfully for industrial telecommunication. It is purely functional with an additional, impure process layer. Processes communicate over implicit, process-global message channels. Erlang is untyped, but has a rich repertoire for dealing with failure. It is not designed for open programming and does not directly support code mobility, but a distinctive feature is code update in active processes.

6.10   OUTLOOK

We presented Alice, a functional language for open programming. Alice provides a novel combination of coherent features to provide concurrency, modularity, a flexible component model and high-level support for distribution. Alice is strongly typed, incorporating a module-based variant of dynamics to embrace openness. It is fully implemented with a rich programming environment

[Ali04], and some small to medium-size demo applications have already been implemented with it, including a distributed constraint solver, a multi-player network game, and a simple framework for web scripting.

There is not yet a formal specification of the full language. Moreover, the implementation does not yet provide extra-lingual safety and security on the level of pickles. To that end, byte code *and* heap need to carry sufficient type information to allow creation of verifiable pickles. It was a deliberate decision to defer research on these issues to future work.

Acknowledgements. We thank our former colleague Leif Kornstaedt, who co-designed Alice and also invested invaluable amounts of work into making it fly.

REFERENCES

[ACPR95]   Martín Abadi, Luca Cardelli, Benjamin Pierce, and Didier Rémy. Dynamic typing in polymorphic languages. *Journal of Functional Programming*, 5(1):111–130, 1995.

[Ali04]   The Alice Project. http://www.ps.uni-sb.de/alice, 2004. Homepage at the Programming Systems Lab, Universität des Saarlandes, Saarbrücken, Germany.

[AVWW96] Joe Armstrong, Robert Virding, Claes Wikström, and Mike Williams. *Concurrent Programming in Erlang, Second Edition*. Prentice-Hall, 1996.

[BK02]   Thorsten Brunklaus and Leif Kornstaedt. A virtual machine for multi-language execution. Technical report, Universität des Saarlandes, Saarbrücken, Germany, 2002.

[DCH03]   Derek Dreyer, Karl Crary, and Robert Harper. A type system for higher-order modules. In *Principles of Programming Languages*, New Orleans, USA, 2003.

[DKSS98]   Denys Duchier, Leif Kornstaedt, Christian Schulte, and Gert Smolka. A higher-order module discipline with separate compilation, dynamic linking, and pickling. Technical report, Universität des Saarlandes, Saarbrücken, Germany, 1998.

[FF95]   Cormac Flanagan and Matthias Felleisen. The semantics of future and its use in program optimizations. In *Principled of Programming Languages*, San Francisco, USA, 1995.

[FMS01]   Cédric Fournet, Luc Maranget, and Alan Schmitt. *The JoCaml Language beta release*. INRIA, http://pauillac.inria.fr/jocaml/htmlman/, 2001.

[GJS96]   James Gosling, Bill Joy, and Guy Steele. *The Java Programming Language Specification*. Addison–Wesley, 1996.

[Hal85]   Robert Halstead. Multilisp: A language for concurrent symbolic computation. *TOPLAS*, 7(4), 1985.

[Ler95]   Xavier Leroy. Applicative functors and fully transparent higher-order modules. In *Principles of Programming Languages*, San Francisco, USA, 1995. ACM.

[Lil97]   Mark Lillibridge. *Translucent Sums: A Foundation for Higher-Order Module Systems*. PhD thesis, Carnegie Mellon University, Pittsburgh, USA, 1997.

[Moz04]   Mozart Consortium.   The Mozart programming system, 2004. www.mozart-oz.org. Accessed 27 April 2005.

[MTHM97]   Robin Milner, Mads Tofte, Robert Harper, and David MacQueen. *Definition of Standard ML (Revised)*. The MIT Press, 1997.

[Myc83]   Alan Mycroft. Dynamic types in ML, 1983. Draft article.

[NSS02]   Joachim Niehren, Jan Schwinghammer, and Gert Smolka. Concurrent computation in a lambda calculus with futures. Technical report, Universität des Saarlandes, 2002.

[Ode05]   Martin Odersky. *Programming in Scala*. École Polytechnique Féd. de Lausanne, 2005.

[Rep99]   John Reppy. *Concurrent Programming in ML*. Cambridge University Press, 1999.

[Rey83]   John Reynolds. Types, abstraction and parametric polymorphism. In *Information Processing*, Amsterdam, 1983. North Holland.

[RLT+04]   Andreas Rossberg, Didier Le Botlan, Guido Tack, Thorsten Brunklaus, and Gert Smolka. Alice through the looking glass (Extended mix). Technical report, Universität des Saarlandes, Saarbrücken, Germany, 2004. http://www.ps.uni-sb.de/Papers/.

[Ros03]   Andreas Rossberg. Generativity and dynamic opacity for abstract types. In *Principles and Practice of Declarative Programming*, Uppsala, Sweden, 2003.

[Ros05]   Andreas Rossberg. The definition of Standard ML with packages. Technical report, Universität des Saarlandes, Saarbrücken, Germany, 2005. http://www.ps.uni-sb.de/Papers/. Accessed 27 April 2005.

[Rus98]   Claudio Russo. *Types for Modules*. Dissertation, University of Edinburgh, 1998.

[Rus00]   Claudio Russo. First-class structures for Standard ML. In In *European Symposium on Programming (ESOP)*, LNCS 1782, pages 336–350. Springer, Berlin.

[SLW+04]   Peter Sewell, James J. Leifer, Keith Wansbrough, Mair Allen-Williams, Francesco Zappa Nardelli, Pierre Habouzit, and Viktor Vafeiadis. Acute: High-level programming language design for distributed computation. Technical Report RR-5329, INRIA, 2004.

[Smo95]   Gert Smolka. The Oz programming model. In *Computer Science Today*, volume 1000 of *LNCS*. Springer-Verlag, Berlin, 1995.

[Tac03]   Guido Tack. Linearisation, minimisation and transformation of data graphs with transients. Diploma thesis, Programming Systems Lab, Universität des Saarlandes, 2003.

[VH04]   Peter Van Roy and Seif Haridi. *Concepts, Techniques, and Models of Computer Programming*. MIT Press, 2004.

Chapter 7

Experiments with GHC's Optimiser

László Németh[1]

Abstract: There are several tricky aspects of compiling a functional language: what optimisations to perform, how to do them efficiently, and when, or more precisely in what order, the optimisations should be done. The literature discussing the first question is abundant, for the second is somewhat sparse and for the third is almost non-existent.

This paper uses the Glasgow Haskell Compiler (GHC) to investigate when the optimisations should be performed to gain maximum benefits, where maximum benefits is defined as shortest runtime, for a given set of optimisations. We focus on GHC, because it has been developed as a test bed for compiler research, but we stress that the techniques are applicable to any other compiler for a functional language.

7.1 INTRODUCTION

The optimising part of compilers is an area where theory and practice rarely meet: the first hardly reaches the complexities (non-confluent rewrite rules, undecidable properties as side conditions) involved in compiling a practical language, the second fails to penetrate its depth because the sequence of transformations that take place can only be followed on small chunks of code. On larger examples unexpected interactions take place which manifest itself by a program going much slower (or faster!) and/or allocating a lot more memory after an innocent change to the source or to the compiler or to the runtime system [Wad87].

The difficulty lies in the large number of ways even a few optimisations can be combined. Furthermore, a program transformation may prove to be an optimisation only if other transformations are also used and the order of the two

---

[1]Department of Computer Science, Bilgi University, Kurtuluşderesi Caddesi No: 47 Dolapdere 34440 Istanbul, Turkey; E-mail: `lnemeth@cs.bilgi.edu.tr`

transformations is right.

In this paper, we describe a method to explore a large subset of the entire search space: using exhaustive search combined with a handful of constraints we are able to systematically generate all versions of a few programs, examine all the steps of their compilation, their run time and total allocation. From this data we are able to justify conjectures, suggest better sequences, and revisit transformations which have previously been considered uncommon.

7.2 CONTRIBUTIONS OF THE PAPER

Better sequences. We demonstrate the existence of optimisation sequences which not only produce faster code on a range of programs but at the same time compile faster.

Feasibility of the approach. Using cheap hardware and networks, plus some reasonable constraints on the search space we show that the search for better optimisation can be done exhaustively.

Folklore. We compare and contrast the good sequences with previous claims about ordering of the optimisation passes. Some claims turn out to be justified while others appear to be unfounded in the light of our comparisons.

Thorough test of the compiler. With the exhaustive search for better sequences we subjected GHC to a thorough test which exposed bugs both in the specialisation and the common-subexpression passes. Once all the benchmarks compile all possible ways the trust in the correctness of the compiler will increase.

7.3 THE SETUP

7.3.1 Language and implementation

Haskell is a polymorphically typed, lazy, purely functional programming language widely used as a test bed for research. The Glasgow Haskell Compiler (GHC) [GHC] is a highly optimising 'industrial-strength' compiler for Haskell. The compiler itself is written in Haskell and it is widely considered to be the fastest available implementation of a lazy functional language. The speed of its compiled code is due to a range of optimisations [PJ96] and aggressive inlining [PJM92] GHC performs on a pure, explicitly-typed, intermediate representation of the program called *Core*.

Some of the Core-to-Core transformations are global, module-at-a-time passes, such as strictness analysis [PJP93], or let-floating [PJPS96]. A handful of other transformations, like `case` based transformations and beta-reduction, are purely local, and are collected together into a single pass called the *simplifier*. It is not easy to generate 'clean' code, e.g. no dead code, while in the midst of a complicated global pass, so the simplifier is also used to clean up (drop dead code) after global transformations.

The local transformations implemented by the simplifier often cascade: inlining, for example, can expose opportunities for certain case transformations, which in turn can make a call site more attractive for further inlining. The occurrence analysis/simplify pass is therefore iterated until the simplifier indicates that no transformations occur or some arbitrary limit (currently 4) is reached.

In contrast to the vast number of suggested optimisations for lazy functional languages, GHC achieves its performance with only eight global transformations. Two of the transformation passes are concerned with the placement of let bindings: floating outwards (CoreDoFloatOutwards aka full-laziness) increases the scope of let bindings to maximise sharing while floating inwards (CoreDoFloatInwards), almost the exact opposite, decreases the scope in the hope that certain allocations can be avoided. Specialisation (CoreDoSpecialising) eliminates overloading by generating monomorphic versions of polymorphic functions at predescribed types. Strictness analysis (CoreDoStrictness) and the worker-wrapper transformation (CoreDoWorkerWrapper) go hand-in-hand: the first annotates functions with strictness properties, the second exploits the annotation by splitting the body into a (possibly large) worker and a small, therefore inlineable, wrapper. Common-subexpression elimination (CoreCSE) is the same as in imperative languages. Case-liberation (CoreLiberateCase) unrolls recursion to allow evaluations to be lifted from a loop, and finally there is (CoreDoSpecConstr) which specialises recursive functions over constructors so certain arguments of a function can be passed unboxed.

These passes can be run in any order, as many times as it is considered necessary. When instructed to optimise (-O2 on the command-line) the compiler performs a sequence of length 18 of these passes as shown in Table 7.1.

7.4   THE METHOD

We systematically generate all sequences of the passes (7 out of the 8 excluding constructor specialisation) between length 5 and 12. This brute force approach gives rise to an enormous ($\sum_{n=5}^{12} 7^n$) number of possible sequences. Most sequences are fortunately meaningless:

- The global, module-at-a-time passes alter the code depending on a set of conditions which do not change during compilation (some of which can be tweaked on the command-line), and there is no random element – like randomly rearranging the order of two lets – involved. Consequently, after a single run of a given pass, since the side conditions do not change, the second pass would find nothing to do.

- The simplifier's activities can also be influenced on the command-line, but as we mentioned earlier, a simplifier run means iterate until fixpoint or a predefined limit (4 iterations) is reached. A second run, at the same inlining phase, has nothing to do.

CoreDoSimplify Gently 4	one pass (which is allowed to iterate four times) of gentle simplification in which very little inlining [PJM92] takes place. The case-of-case transformation is disabled
CoreDoSpecialising	
CoreDoFloatOutwards False False	full-laziness with floating of lambdas and constants are disabled
CoreDoFloatInwards	moves `let`'s inwards in the hope of avoiding allocation
CoreDoSimplify 2 4	simplification with inline phase 2, with a maximum of four iterations
CoreDoSimplify 1 4	another pass of simplification, with more aggressive inlining
CoreDoSimplify 0 4	simplification. All identifiers are allowed to be inlined with the exception of those which are specifically marked NoInline
CoreDoStrictness	annotates identifiers with strictness information
CoreDoWorkerWrapper	worker-wrapper split
CoreDoGlomBinds	is not an optimisation on its own right as it lumps together lets to a big letrec
CoreDoSimplify 0 4	simplification at phase 0
CoreDoFloatOutwards False True	another pass of full-laziness, this time allowing constants to be floated outwards
CoreCSE	common-subexpression elimination
CoreDoFloatInwards	
CoreDoSimplify 0 4	
CoreLiberateCase	case liberation
CoreDoSpecConstr	constructor specialisation
CoreDoSimplify 0 4	final simplification

TABLE 7.1.   Current sequence of optimisations for `-O2` in GHC

Imposing the following constraints on the sequences cuts down the number dramatically to 43680 for 7 passes[2] of length $5 - 12$.

- No consecutive runs of the same pass: the global transformations and the simplifier do as much as they can in one pass and afterwards there are no more opportunities for the same transformation.

- The worker-wrapper transformation is run immediately after strictness analysis as this ordering gives the most benefit: strictness is an analysis and the worker-wrapper transformation only exploits its results. It is not meaningless to run the worker-wrapper pass without strictness analysis or to allow other transformations to take place as some transformations can 'manually' annotate functions with strictness information, but it is very unlikely to be more beneficial.

- Simplifier phases form a non-increasing sequence: counting downwards from phase 2 to phase 0 (inline all identifiers). GHC already follows this rule.

---

[2]For all 8 passes the number of meaningful sequences is 755370, which requires almost 20 times more work, but still manageable.

- The simplifier is allowed to run a maximum of 10 iterations instead of 4. This
  ensures that we never have to run two passes of the simplifier consecutively
  with the same phase.

The limits are arbitrary: any sequence under length 5 is unlikely to be optimising
on a sufficiently wide range on programs, and 12 was chosen to control the time
it takes to run the experiments.

The generated sequences are used to compile the benchmark programs. The
standard libraries are not recompiled.

7.4.1 Benchmark suite

The `nofib` [Par92] suite of Haskell programs is a large collection of programs
which is generally used for benchmarking. The suite is organised into three sets:
the imaginary part contains small programs which are rarely true indicators of
the optimising abilities of a compiler. The spectral subset has somewhat larger
programs, and in some cases can be used to test whether an optimisation is worth
the effort. Finally the real subset has programs that were written to get a job
done. The programs are usually of reasonable size, and none have trivial input or
behaviour.

All the six programs of Table 7.2 come from the real part of the `nofib` suite
and were chosen to allow a rough comparison – by reporting speedups for the
very same programs – of our method, which can be seen as a relatively high
level optimisation, to that of Mycroft [NM02] who examined how much speed
improvement can be gained by paying attention to the cache behaviour of lazy
functional programs. The two approaches otherwise are complementary.

While the programs are unmodified, their inputs were chosen so that runtimes
are not too short.

We believe the question whether the chosen benchmarks are representative
(of programs that get written in Haskell?) to be somewhat misguided since it
suggests the existence of a sequence of optimisations which can compile any code
'optimally', say to run not slower than 5% of the runtime of the best sequence
for a given set of transformations. While it might be possible to construct such a
simplifier, for example by making all known exceptions a special case with special
side conditions, it is not very desirable: the code which implements it would likely
to be horrendously complicated and unmaintainable and it would not deepen our
understanding of what constitutes a good sequence.

Instead, we suggest that the compiler should *adapt* its sequence of optimisations to the code being compiled based on some syntactic or semantic criteria.
Consider, for example, the difference between compiling library code versus the
main module of an application with respect to specialisation. At the time of compiling the code which is destined to be a library it is rarely known what monomorphic instances will be required. So instead of not specialising at all or generating
all the frequently used instances the code should be compiled in such a way that
it is *prepared* to be specialised at a later stage without missing possibilities of optimisation. We do not pursue these ideas any further, but it appears that the brute

Program	Description	Lines	Runtime -O2
anna	Frontier-based strictness analyser	5740	26.30s
compress2	Text compression	147	0.36s
fulsom	Solid modeller	857	1.02s
hidden	PostScript polygon renderer	362	1.62s
infer	Hindley-Milner type inference	561	10.40s
scs	Set circuit simulator	585	3.10s

TABLE 7.2.   Benchmarks used

force approach of this paper is an appropriate tool in finding distinct classes of programs and their optimisation sequences.

7.4.2   Compilation

The benchmarks were compiled, using the same modified version of GHC 6.2.2, on a network of practically identical[3] machines: Pentium IV 2.66GHz, 512KB cache, 512MB RAM, connected thorough 100MBps Ethernet, running a recent version of Debian Linux with kernel 2.4.23.

Using the optimisation options of the fastest contenders on each individual machine programs were recompiled on a machine not connected to any type of network and rerun (3 times, and the average is taken) to ensure comparable results.

7.5   EVALUATION

Feasibility of the brute force approach hinges on four issues: (1) space and time requirements of compiling the programs all the required ways; (2) the time it takes to select the best performers on each machine plus the time it takes to recompile and rerun the candidates on a single machine for comparable runtimes; (3) the existence of 'better' sequences; and finally (4) the applicability of these good sequences to other programs. We examine these four issues in turn.

7.5.1   Space and time requirement

Compiling the six benchmark programs 43680 different ways takes about 15 hours on 50 computers, which is not unreasonable. The size of the log files of the compilation, which include the sequence of the passes, statistics about the simplifier, and the final simplified version of each module in Core (which is not necessary for the purposes of this paper) is large (1MB+) but compresses extremely well with the Burrows-Wheeler block sorting algorithm of bzip2. The size of the compressed

---

[3]Being 'practically identical' is not very important as long as the machines are the same architecture, because the fastest, selected versions are recompiled and rerun on the same machine. The machines were of identical hardware specification, supplied by one manufacturer around the same date, and had identical software installed. See Section 7.5.2.

logs varies between 20-150KB. Stripped executables, also compressed, are about 100K. Log files of the actual runs, which include basic information about total allocation and the output of the `time` command are tiny, approximately 350 bytes. This puts the overall space requirement to around 80GB for the six benchmarks.

Neither the space nor the time requirements are excessive. Adding a dozen more benchmarks or a few more optimisation passes is still manageable. Space can be saved by not logging the final simplified version of each module and/or deleting the executables if compilation is interleaved with running the benchmarks.

7.5.2 Recompilation and benchmarking

While our method is essentially an exhaustive search the results (especially run times) from different machines are not directly comparable. To ensure valid comparison we choose (the sequences of) the top performers from each machine and then recompile the programs on one machine.

There are various ways the best candidates on each machine can be chosen. Whatever the choice is the main limitation is that the chosen programs should compile and run on a single machine in reasonable time. We found that on average a Pentium IV can compile about 250 programs (of our chosen benchmarks) per hour.

1. We can take the top n performers with a fixed n. For m machines and b benchmarks this gives $n * m * b$ compilations. Recompiling the top 20 performers is a day's work.

2. We can compile and run the six benchmark programs on each machine with GHC's current optimisation sequence (`-O2`) and choose all those programs which are faster. Approximately, 5% of the generated sequences (2000 programs out of 43680) make the benchmarks go faster than `-O2`. Recompilation is about two day's work.

We currently use the first option as the second one is generally a lot more work unless there are few sequences better than `-O2`.

The time to rerun all the benchmarks is considerably less than the time it takes to compile them, even when the inputs are suitably modified.

7.5.3 Good sequences

Table 7.3 lists the actual speedups for all six programs for the best sequence of the given benchmark. As expected, there is no sequence which makes all the programs fastest and there is only one (see Section 7.5.4) which puts all six benchmarks into the top ten. Approximately 1% of the sequences make all benchmarks perform in the top one hundred, all of which beats `-O2`. Unfortunately, the difference of the averages across the benchmarks is so little – well below for example the accuracy of the `time` command we use to measure the runtime – that it is

Program	Runtime -O2	Fastest (% of -O2)	Slowest	Unoptimised -Onot
anna	26.30s	25.01 (95%)	31.02	30.59
compress2	0.36s	0.32 (88%)	0.55	0.60
fulsom	1.02s	0.91 (89%)	1.51	1.76
hidden	1.62s	1.55 (95%)	3.40	7.27
infer	10.40s	9.56 (91%)	12.20	17.78
scs	3.10s	2.85 (91%)	3.50	6.48

TABLE 7.3.   Best and worst performers

impossible to identify a single sequence as the best. The table shows modest, but not negligible improvements. As the slowest performers are much slower than -O2 it also shows that GHC's sequence is impressively tuned.

Table 7.3 is not without surprises: anna for example when compared to unoptimised code gets slower after optimisation. Fortunately this happens with only one sequence.

Sequences in Table 7.4, which gives a random identifier, the length of the sequence, the sequence itself and a short remark, come from the top 100 performers, and all of them are faster than -O2. They were randomly chosen to demonstrate that widely differing sequences are amongst the best. There are number of points worth noting about the entries:

- Full-laziness (FloatOutwards) generally comes late, despite the observation of Santos [San95] and the current practice in GHC (Table 7.1) that it should happen before any inlining takes place.

- CSE features rather frequently (253 out of 292 examined) despite Chitil's claim [Chi97] that common-subexpressions are uncommon in a lazy functional programs. Because of the exhaustiveness of the search (for all sequences with CSE one without it was run and did not make it to the top) we can make a strong claim: CSE does make (a yet unquantified) difference.

- The number of simplifier passes varies from as little as three to six, not counting the initial 'Gentle' pass.

- One of the best performers is only of length 11, which compares well with GHC's current sequence of length 18.

- Strictness analysis and the worker-wrapper transformation appears in all the top performers, though its placement varies considerably.

A more refined analysis of groups of 'good' and 'bad' sequences have been attempted through searching for longest common subsequences and other similarity measures over sequences but none of them proved to be conclusive so far. A detailed study of good and bad sequences for space behaviour (total allocation, lag, drag, and void) is the subject of a forthcoming paper.

ID	(length) Options	Remark
nipwxc	(11) Simplify, FloatInwards, Simplify 2, FloatOutwards, Specialising, Simplify 1, Strictness, WorkerWrapper, LiberateCase, Simplify 0, CSE	short sequence, late CSE
rYfleO	(14) Simplify, Specialising, Simplify 2, LiberateCase, Simplify 1, CSE, Simplify 0, FloatInwards, Simplify 0, FloatOutwards, Simplify 0, Strictness, WorkerWrapper, CoreDoSimplify 0	full-laziness after inlining
kgbeGv	(11) Simplify, Specialising, Strictness, WorkerWrapper, Simplify 2, LiberateCase, Simplify 1, CSE, FloatInwards, Simplify 0, FloatOutwards	late full-lazines
TMM95z	(11) Simplify, LiberateCase, FloatInwards, Simplify 2, FloatOutwards, Simplify 1, CSE, Simplify 0, Strictness, WorkerWrapper, Simplify 0	no specialisation
r4qQTC	(13) Simplify, CSE, Simplify 2, LiberateCase, Simplify 1, Specialising, Simplify 0, FloatOutwards, Simplify 0, Strictness, WorkerWrapper, FloatInwards, Simplify 0	early CSE
NtmAht	(12) Simplify, Specialising, Simplify 2, Strictness, WorkerWrapper, Simplify 1, LiberateCase, Simplify 0, FloatInwards, FloatOutwards, Simplify 0, CoreCSE	floating in is not followed by simplification
zPYd7H	(14) Simplify, Specialising, Simplify 2, CSE, Simplify 1, LiberateCase, Simplify 0, FloatInwards, Simplify 0 10, FloatOutwards, Simplify 0, Strictness, WorkerWrapper, CoreDoSimplify 0	floating in before strictness
HP0d25	(12) Simplify, FloatOutwards, FloatInwards, Simplify 2, Specialising, Simplify 1, CSE, Simplify 0, LiberateCase, Strictness, WorkerWrapper, Simplify 0	the only early full-laziness
N0vZ5h	(13) Simplify, Strictness, WorkerWrapper, Simplify 2, CSE, Simplify 1, LiberateCase, Simplify 0, Specialising, Simplify 0 10, FloatOutwards, FloatInwards, Simplify 0	very early strictness
tYHSxT	(11) Simplify, Specialising, FloatInwards, LiberateCase, Simplify 2, CSE, FloatOutwards, Simplify 1, Strictness, WorkerWrapper, Simplify 0	late strictness

TABLE 7.4.   Ten sequences better than `-O2`

7.5.4   How general are they?

So far comparisons have been limited to other programs from the `nofib` suite. While this is not ideal it does give an indication about the generality of the sequences which were derived from only six programs. Table 7.5 and 7.6 summarises our findings and they can be interpreted as follows. In the first column the name of the benchmark program appears. For each program five rows of data are presented: the first row (`-O2`) gives details about compiling the given benchmark with `-O2`. The second row gives the name of two sequences which minimise/maximise the size of the generated code (the third column). The third row shows min/max values of compilation time (the fourth column), the fourth shows min/max values of total allocation and so on. As these extremal values do not necessarily coincide for a given sequence (there is no guarantee that the compiled code size and the compile time and the total allocation and the runtime are minimum or maximum for a given sequence) the minimum/maximum relationship between the numbers of an entry only holds in the diagonal where the items are highlighted: in other columns the first/second number shows the allocation, run time etc. of the sequence. For example, the fourth entry for `circsim` in Table 7.5 which starts `HP0d25`/`kgbeGv` says that the sequence `HP0d25` makes `circsim` allocate the least amount (612358260) bytes of memory while the other sequence `kgbeGv` makes it allocate the most (641035716) for the sequences of Table 7.4. Note, that the sequences in Table 7.4 were chosen to demonstrate that widely differing options generate fast code and not to show the very best performers in each category. The meaning of columns is self explanatory: the first (Sequence) gives the name of the sequence from Table 7.4 which was used to compile the program. Consequent columns can be grouped to (1) compile time information giving the size of the code (denoted Size) and compilation time (Compile), (2) runtime information giving the total allocation (Alloc) and the total runtime of the program (Run).

Within the six programs of Table 7.3 the length 11 sequence 'Simplify, Float-Inwards, Simplify 2, Strictness, WorkerWrapper, Simpify 1, LiberateCase, Simpify 0, CSE, FloatOutwards, Simpify 0' (which does not appear in Table 7.4) makes all six programs perform in the top ten. While the existence of such sequence is encouraging, there is no guarantee that the same sequence will not make another program run far worse than with `-O2`.

Comparing the good sequences to other programs gives somewhat mixed results. Table 7.5 and 7.6 shows twenty-two programs[4] from all three parts (imaginary, spectral, and real) of the `nofib` suite. For most programs the better sequences found only examining six programs do give improvements. The top sequences still perform well for `cacheprof` and `symalg` (both from the real subset), though the speedups are not as great as in Table 7.3. On the other hand none of the top sequences make `circsim` run as fast as with `-O2` and in general the gap between the best of the top ten and `-O2` is much narrower ($< 2\%$). This can be attributed to several different causes: either the sequences derived for the six real benchmarks are not general and possibly do not generalise well, or a larger set of programs must be used to find better sequences or GHC's optimisation sequence is fine tuned to the spectral subset of the `nofib` suite. All three explanations are plausible and warrant further investigation.

There are real surprises as well: the sequence `HP0d25` makes `constraints` run 25% faster despite that at the same time it also makes it allocate most. It is unclear whether `-O2` misses an opportunity or a bug in the compiler perhaps triggers possibilities of further optimisation.

7.6   RELATED WORK

There have been a number of attempts at meta optimisation, optimising the optimiser of compilers. The first thorough study for lazy functional languages on the

---

[4]Results for the entire `nofib` and detailed analysis of optimisation on the code of small programs can be found in the extended version of this paper.

effect of individual transformations on the quality of the code was conducted by Santos and reported in his thesis [San95]. His results were derived by studiously examining large chunks of core programs and fine tuning both the transformations, that is the side conditions on the rewrite rules, and their sequence. His method is inherently limited as optimisations interact unexpectedly.

Realising that 'eyeballing' large amounts of optimised code is not feasible, for imperative languages Pugh's Unified Transformation Framework (UTF) [KP93] allows searching the entire optimisation space. Based on UTF, machine learning techniques have been employed to effectively search for better sequences [LO04].

Closely related is iterative compilation [KKO02], where the compiler repeatedly executes different versions of the code and uses the feedback to decide the next optimisation attempt.

All these approaches suffer from the same limitation: none can prove definitively that for a given set of optimisations the one found is the best for a class of programs or a given program.

7.7 CONCLUSIONS

This paper has revisited an ancient approach to meta optimisation, previously seen as computationally infeasible. With the addition of sensible constraints on the optimisation space and the increased availability of cheap hardware and networks, the method has been demonstrated to be viable.

We not only found better sequences of optimisation passes which make programs compile and run faster at the same time, almost as a side effect we subjected GHC to the most thorough test of thousands of compilations with different optimisations. Several bugs in the specialisation and common-subexpression elimination pass showed up. Once eliminated, the absence of these bugs will increase our trust in the compiler.

Future work is needed in several directions. The main bottleneck of our approach is the recompilation and rerunning of the benchmarks on a single machine to ensure comparable results. Thorough statistical approaches it appears to be possible to extend benchmarking on a single machine to a number of machines while ensuring that run times remain comparable. Doing so will further expand our ability to search for longer and even better sequences of optimisations.

Analysis of the results should be put on a more solid theoretical basis to see if the measured differences are statistically significant and due to the optimisation sequence or other factors.

Our main concern in this experiment was to minimise run time of the optimised programs. The analysis should be repeated for space consumption and it would be interesting to explore whether our findings can be correlated to Sands' improvement theory [MS99, GS01].

Most importantly perhaps, there is very little understanding why the newly discovered optimisation sequences work better than the one currently used by GHC. Perhaps this thorough study will open up new avenues for understanding optimisation and optimising compilers.

Acknowledgements. Many thanks to Simon Marlow who prompted me to generate Table 7.5 and 7.6 and in doing so made me write my most elaborate awk scripts to date, and to Chris Stephenson for a thorough review of the paper.

REFERENCES

[Chi97]   Olaf Chitil. Common subexpressions are uncommon in lazy functional languages. In Chris Clack, Tony Davie, and Kevin Hammond, editors, *Proceedings of the 9th International Workshop on Implementation of Functional Languages, St. Andrews, Scotland*, LNCS 1467, pages 53–71, 1997. Springer Verlag, Berlin.

[GHC]   The Glasgow Haskell Compiler. http://www.haskell.org/ghc. Accessed 27 April 2005.

[GS01]   Jörgen Gustavsson and David Sands. Possibilities and limitations of call-by-need space improvement. In *Proceeding of the Sixth ACM SIGPLAN International Conference on Functional Programming (ICFP'01)*, pages 265–276. ACM Press, September 2001.

[KKO02]   P. M. W. Knijnenburg, T. Kisuki, and M. F. P. O'Boyle. Iterative compilation. In *Embedded processor design challenges: systems, architectures, modeling, and simulation-SAMOS*, pages 171–187. Springer-Verlag New York, 2002.

[KP93]   Wayne Kelly and William Pugh. A framework for unifying reordering transformations. Technical Report CS-TR-3193, Dept of CS, University of Maryland, 1993.

[LO04]   Shun Long and Michael O'Boyle. Adaptive java optimisation using instance-based learning. In *Proceedings of the 18th annual international conference on Supercomputing*, pages 237–246. ACM Press, 2004.

[MS99]   A. K. Moran and D. Sands. Improvement in a lazy context: An operational theory for call-by-need. In *Proc. POPL'99, the 26th ACM SIGPLAN-SIGACT Symposium on Principles of Programming Languages*, pages 43–56. ACM Press, January 1999.

[NM02]   Nicholas Nethercote and Alan Mycroft. The cache behaviour of large lazy functional programs on stock hardware. In *Proceedings of the workshop on Memory system performance*, pages 44–55. ACM Press, 2002.

[Par92]   W. Partain. The nofib benchmark suite of Haskell programs. In J. Launchbury and P. Sansom, editors, *Proceedings of the 1992 Glasgow Workshop on Functional Programming*, pages 195–202, Ayr, Scotland, July 1992. Springer-Verlag.

[PJ96]   Simon L Peyton Jones. Compiling haskell by program transformation: A report from the trenches. In *European Symposium on Programming*, pages 18–44, 1996. Springer Verlag, Berlin.

[PJM92]   Simon Peyton Jones and Simon Marlow. Secrets of the Glasgow Haskell Compiler inliner. *Journal of Functional Programming*, 12(4 & 5):393–434, July & September 1992.

[PJP93]   Simon Peyton-Jones and WD Partain. Measuring the effectiveness of a simple strictness analyser. In K Hammond and JT O'Donnel, editors, *Functional Programming*, Workshops in Computing, pages 201–220. Springer Verlag, Berlin, 1993.

[PJPS96]   Simon Peyton Jones, Will Partain, and André Santos. Let-floating: Moving bindings to give faster programs. In *International Conference on Functional Programming*, pages 1–12, 1996. ACM Press.

[San95]   André Santos. *Compilation by transformation in non-strict functional languages*. PhD thesis, Department of Computing Science, Glasgow University, 1995.

[Wad87]   Philip Wadler. Fixing some space leaks with a garbage collector. *Software Practice and Experience*, 17(9):595–608, Sep 1987.

Program	Sequence	Size	Compile	Alloc	Run
	-O2	242889	1.02	62860	0.03
	nipwxc/TMM95z	**241833/243689**	0.83/0.99	62892/62992	0.03/0.01
ansi	nipwxc/TMM95z	241833/243689	**0.83/0.99**	62892/62992	0.03/0.01
	TMM95z/HP0d25	243689/243545	0.99/0.94	**62892/63053**	0.01/0.01
	TMM95z/r4qQTC	243689/242313	0.99/0.90	62892/62932	**0.01/0.03**
	-O2	350644	1.11	205663808	0.53
	TMM95z/zPYd7H	**348580/350676**	0.90/1.11	229581708/205663808	0.58/0.51
atom	TMM95z/kgbeGv	348580/350212	**0.90/1.17**	229581708/205663808	0.58/0.50
	N0vZ5h/TMM95z	348820/348580	0.95/0.90	**205663808/229581708**	0.52/0.57
	NtmAht/TMM95z	350900/348580	1.09/0.90	205663808/229581708	**0.49/0.57**
	-O2	196816	1.29	128972	0.01
	TMM95z/zPYd7H	**197232/192344**	1.28/1.33	129576/129576	0.02/0.02
awards	nipwxc/rYfleO	197296/197344	**1.25/1.34**	132588/129576	0.01/0.02
	HP0d25/kgbeGv	197232/197344	1.31/1.31	**129576/133256**	0.01/0.01
	HP0d25/zPYd7H	197232/192344	1.31/1.33	129576/129576	**0.01/0.02**
	-O2	254106	1.57	122296	0.02
	HP0d25/NtmAht	**254106/265034**	1.56/2.13	127136/127016	0.01/0.02
banner	HP0d25/zPYd7H	254106/265018	**1.56/2.21**	127136/132968	0.01/0.02
	HP0d25/N0vZ5h	254106/265018	1.56/2.17	**122320/132968**	0.01/0.02
	kgbeGv/zPYd7H	254394/265018	1.61/2.21	127088/132968	**0.01/0.02**
	-O2	209728	3.07	27398256	0.07
	TMM95z/nipwxc	**213520/232272**	2.98/3.83	27398792/27398792	0.09/0.09
boyer	kgbeGv/nipwxc	213056/232272	**2.86/3.83**	27399804/27398792	0.09/0.09
	HP0d25/kgbeGv	213520/213056	3.05/2.86	**27398792/27399804**	0.07/0.09
	rYfleO/nipwxc	218224/232272	3.21/3.83	27399776/27398792	**0.07/0.09**
	-O2	226464	4.19	1796060	0.03
	TMM95z/kgbeGv	**225552/226640**	4.09/4.06	1796060/1800908	0.04/0.04
boyer2	NtmAht/r4qQTC	226272/226192	**4.03/4.15**	1796060/1796060	0.04/0.04
	HP0d25/kgbeGv	225568/226640	4.13/4.06	**1796060/1800908**	0.03/0.04
	N0vZ5h/kgbeGv	226032/226640	4.14/4.06	1800908/1800908	**0.02/0.04**
	-O2	319958	4.43	623303904	1.88
	HP0d25/NtmAht	**319782/330310**	4.23/4.88	634884716/626695220	2.42/2.34
circsim	kgbeGv/NtmAht	321734/330310	**4.16/4.88**	641035716/626695229	2.43/2.34
	HP0d25/kgbeGv	319782/321734	4.23/4.16	**612358260/641035716**	2.42/2.43
	N0vZ5h/TMM95z	321942/323526	4.38/4.42	612358260/641027996	**2.26/2.48**
	-O2	289510	2.34	947010684	7.49
	N0vZ5h/nipwxc	**287686/289654**	2.11/2.20	956680152/966636052	7.45/7.60
constraints	kgbeGv/rYfleO	287830/298110	**2.10/2.33**	956655892/963429740	7.52/7.64
	kgbeGv/HP0d25	287830/289382	2.10/2.27	**956655892/1086116140**	7.52/5.45
	HP0d25/TMM95z	289382/289254	2.27/2.23	1086116140/966636052	**5.45/7.69**
	-O2	180368	0.55	934799436	2.18
	nipwxc/zPYd7H	**180128/180256**	0.54/0.57	979131900/934799436	2.23/2.18
crypta1	nipwxc/r4qQTC	180128/180256	**0.54/0.58**	979131900/934799436	2.23/2.18
	HP0d25/kgbeGv	180160/180208	0.55/0.55	**934799436/979131900**	2.21/2.23
	r4qQTC/nipwxc	180256/180128	0.58/0.54	934799436/979131900	**2.18/2.23**
	-O2	202300	2.47	176013164	1.11
	TMM95z/NtmAht	**201820/202412**	2.34/2.31	176013992/176013884	1.09/1.10
wave4main	kgbeGv/r4qQTC	202396/202300	**2.28/2.44**	216264584/183294744	1.37/1.16
	HP0d25/N0vZ5h	201964/202332	2.40/2.34	**176013132/216264584**	1.10/1.37
	TMM95z/kgbeGv	201820/202396	2.34/2.28	176013992/216264584	**1.09/1.37**
	-O2	301168	10.83	312752216	0.77
	TMM95z/NtmAht	**293296/314176**	9.55/10.80	315698208/315018004	0.75/0.74
transform	TMM95z/NtmAht	293296/314176	**9.55/10.80**	315698208/315018004	0.75/0.74
	N0vZ5h/nipwxc	300304/313360	10.29/10.27	**309823768/316132848**	0.75/0.78
	NtmAht/kgbeGv	314174/301984	10.80/9.73	315018004/309823768	**0.74/0.81**

TABLE 7.5.   Other programs with the best sequences (imaginary, spectral)

Program	Sequence	Size	Compile	Alloc	Run
	-O2	208816	3.25	154159284	0.65
	TMM95z/NtmAht	**208848/217664**	3.19/3.62	155107528/154686232	0.64/0.65
typecheck	HP0d25/NtmAht	208928/217664	**3.14/3.62**	154698364/155107528	0.64/0.65
	rYfleO/N0vZ5h	209216/213200	3.26/3.46	**154043644/169173192**	0.66/0.72
	zPYd7H/kgbeGv	212400/210208	3.46/3.18	154047868/169169096	**0.62/0.74**
	-O2	546661	13.43	256395112	1.63
	N0vZ5h/NtmAht	**531525/553797**	11.84/13.71	289003432/270380460	1.68/1.62
simple	kgbeGv/NtmAht	531989/553797	**11.17/13.71**	287004124/270380460	1.75/1.62
	HP0d25/N0vZ5h	541253/531525	12.67/11.84	**256333652/289003432**	1.63/1.68
	nipwxc/kgbeGv	549125/531989	13.25/11.17	270302344/287004124	**1.56/1.76**
	-O2	1034482	64.27	315200696	26.97
	TMM95z/NtmAht	**977074/1036674**	57.84/61.68	321941404/319535068	27.09/27.01
anna	TMM95z/nipwxc	977074/1031026	**57.84/120.15**	321941494/319408952	27.09/26.94
	HP0d25/TMM95z	1010066/977074	60.34/57.84	**315361796/321941404**	26.82/27.27
	HP0d25/rYfleO	1010066/1002354	60.34/61.73	315361796/318167136	**26.82/27.42**
	-O2	622199	27.79	223058784	1.12
	TMM95z/NtmAht	**607603/821623**	23.24/34.39	231340688/-	1.02/-
cacheprof	TMM95z/NtmAht	607603/821623	**23.24/34.39**	231340688/-	1.02/-
	HP0d25/N0vZ5h	610935/630279	25.59/24.99	**223885704/238472532**	1.02/1.03
	r4qQTC/zPYd7H	627543/627447	25.23/25.73	231828152/231234160	**0.99/1.05**
	-O2	284217	2.92	50795796	0.35
	r4qQTC/nipwxc	**273417/275577**	2.15/2.17	52312884/52299612	0.36/0.35
compress2	kgbeGv/NtmAht	274073/275449	**2.04/2.20**	52312940/52312884	0.36/0.36
	HP0d25/N0vZ5h	273529/273705	2.08/2.10	**52299612/52312940**	0.35/0.36
	TMM95z/N0vZ5h	273529/273705	2.09/2.10	52299612/52312940	**0.33/0.36**
	-O2	504500	15.59	189644804	0.90
	kgbeGv/nipwxc	**493588/542180**	14.07/16.73	236125632/205597488	1.06/0.89
fulsom	kgbeGv/NtmAht	493588/540628	**14.07/17.14**	236125632/193704524	1.06/0.89
	r4qQTC/kgbeGv	509268/493588	15.58/14.07	**188916744/236125632**	0.87/1.06
	rYfleO/kgbeGv	504452/493588	15.37/14.07	193704524/236125632	**0.87/1.08**
	-O2	501159	10.95	554238104	1.53
	TMM95z/NtmAht	**495831/503159**	10.05/10.52	528499288/539923976	1.51/1.53
hidden	N0vZ5h/rYfleO	496135/501047	**9.92/10.66**	543306832/527243308	1.54/1.54
	rYfleO/HP0d25	501047/496455	10.66/10.12	**527243308/554033396**	1.54/1.64
	TMM95z/HP0d25	495831/496455	10.05/1012	528499288/554033396	**1.49/1.65**
	-O2	402918	10.63	129904084	10.73
	TMM95z/nipwxc	**402662/405958**	10.39/10.30	851656892/861338180	10.25/10.71
infer	nipwxc/N0vZ5h	402662/405558	**10.39/10.76**	851656892/862911748	10.25/10.31
	rYfleO/kgbeGv	403334/404662	10.69/10.43	**849057200/863387040**	10.02/9.91
	kgbeGv/HP0d25	404662/405558	10.43/10.33	863387040/850928032	**9.91/10.73**
	-O2	566466	14.26	860833812	3.02
	N0vZ5h/rYfleO	**556164/565266**	12.57/13.89	864031608/864277888	2.92/2.94
scs	N0vZ5h/rYfleO	556164/565266	**12.57/13.89**	864031608/864277888	2.92/2.94
	HP0d25/r4qQTC	565170/565234	13.62/13.59	**860727196/864647380**	2.95/3.08
	rYfleO/r4qQTC	565266/565234	13.89/13.59	864277888/864647380	**2.84/3.08**
	-O2	455687	10.41	5013837920	30.95
	zPYd7H/NtmAht	**463175/473735**	10.67/10.83	5013833836/5013837944	30.78/30.97
symalg	TMM95z/nipwxc	452502/473303	**9.97/10.98**	5013833532/5013833532	30.81/30.96
	HP0d25/r4qQTC	453655/463767	10.29/10.46	**5013833496/5013843700**	31.00/31.04
	zPYd7H/kgbeGv	463175/465463	10.67/10.37	5013833836/5013843564	**30.73/31.26**
	-O2	958570	59.84	521696	0.03
	TMM95z/NtmAht	**925128/1038410**	54.73/60.06	523956/523228	0.01/0.01
veritas	TMM95z/NtmAht	925128/1038410	**54.73/60.06**	523956/523228	0.01/0.01
	rYfleO/HP0d25	966042/937514	58.81/55.97	**523112/527156**	0.02/0.02
	TMM95z/N0vZ5h	925178/974538	54.73/57.61	523956/524248	**0.01/0.03**

TABLE 7.6.   Other programs with the best sequences (spectral, real)

Chapter 8

Disjoint Forms in Graphical User Interfaces

Sander Evers, Peter Achten, Rinus Plasmeijer[1]

Abstract: Forms are parts of a graphical user interface (GUI) that show a (structured) value and allow the user to update it. Some forms express a choice between two or more (structured) values using radio buttons or check boxes. We show that explicitly modelling such a choice leads to a cleaner separation of logic and layout. This is done by extending the combinator library FunctionalForms with *disjoint form combinators*. To implement these, we have generalized the technique of compositional functional references which underlies the library.

8.1 INTRODUCTION

Forms are parts of a graphical user interface (GUI) that show a (structured) value and allow the user to update it. For example, the omnipresent dialogs labelled *Options*, *Settings* and *Preferences* are forms. An address book can also be considered a form. In our previous work, we have developed the combinator library FunctionalForms [EAK05] for building forms in a concise, compositional way.

Many real-life forms allow a choice between two or more alternatives, some of which require extra information. For example, the form in Figure 8.1 indicates whether the user wishes to receive a certain newsletter; if s/he does, the text entry field next to this option should contain his/her e-mail adress. If s/he does not, this text field is irrelevant (some GUIs provide a visual clue for this: the control is dimmed).

Usually, the information in such a form is processed as a product-like data structure containing the choice (e.g. as a boolean) and the extra information (e.g. as a string). However, most functional languages allow data types which are more

---

[1]Radboud University Nijmegen, Department of Software Technology, Toernooiveld 1, 6525 ED Nijmegen, The Netherlands; E-mail:
{s.evers,p.achten,rinus}@cs.ru.nl

FIGURE 8.1.   A 'disjoint' form

suited to this task, namely *disjoint union types*. In Haskell [Pey03], we would
define

data *NewsLetter* = *NewsYes String* | *NewsNo*

for the type of information in the example form.

While the combinators in FunctionalForms previously only supported forms
with product-like data structures, in this paper we extend them to enable the explicit definition of such a *disjoint form*. Rather than as a 'yes/no' form *and* an
'e-mail' form, it can now be composed as a 'yes, e-mail' form *or* a 'no' form.
We demonstrate that this technique leads to a better separation of logic and layout
in disjoint forms. For its implementation, we have generalized the *compositional
functional references* which underlie the library.

This paper is organized as follows: it first gives a summary of the library's
basic use, which has not changed (Section 8.2). Then, the use and merits of the
extension are demonstrated (Section 8.3), after which its implementation is discussed in Section 8.4. Next, we show that the gained flexibility leads to some
safety issues (Section 8.5). We finish with related work (Section 8.6) and conclu-
sions (Section 8.7).

8.2 FUNCTIONALFORMS SUMMARY

FunctionalForms [EAK05] is a combinator library built on the GUI library wx-
Haskell [Lei04] (itself built on the cross-platform C++ library wxWidgets [wxW]).
It can be seen as an embedded domain-specific language for forms: it consists of
atomic forms and ways to combine them into larger forms in a declarative style.
In this section, we give a brief summary of its basic use, which is the same as
described in [EAK05], although the types have changed a little.

A *form* is a GUI part, residing somewhere within a dialog with *OK* and *Cancel*
buttons, which is only able to display and alter a certain value. When the dialog
appears, the form has an *initial value* which is provided by its environment; subsequently, the user can read and alter this value; at the end, the user closes the
dialog with one of the buttons, and the form passes the *final value* back to the
environment. The type of this value is called the *subject type* of the form.

Atomic forms correspond to a single control containing an editable value. Examples are a text entry field, containing a *String*, and a spin control, containing an
Int:

FIGURE 8.2. *ticketsForm*

entry′ :: *Monad m* ⇒
    [*Prop* (*TextCtrl* ())] → *Ref m String* → *FForm win m Layout*
spinCtrl′ :: *Monad m* ⇒
    Int → *Int* → [*Prop* (*SpinCtrl* ())] → *Ref m Int* → *FForm win m Layout*

We follow the convention that library functions are underlined, and an atomic form is named after the corresponding wxHaskell function which creates its control, but with an additional prime symbol. Every atomic form is parameterized with a list of optional properties used for customizing the control, e.g. its size and font (leaving this list empty produces reasonable defaults). Some atomic forms, like *spinCtrl′*, require additional parameters: its first two arguments indicate a minimum and maximum value.

All these parameters actually have little to do with FunctionalForms: they are directly passed to the wxHaskell control creation function. In contrast, the last parameter of both forms is specific to FunctionalForms; it is a *reference value* which relates the atomic form's subject type (*String* and *Int*, respectively) to the subject type of the top-level form. A more detailed description of the *Ref* and *FForm* types is postponed to Section 8.4.

To combine atomic forms into larger forms, two aspects have to be composed: layout and subject type. The former is performed by *layout combinators* like *grid′*, *margin′* and *floatLeft′*. These are based on the wxHaskell layout combinators after which they are named, but operate directly on forms.[1] For example, the two atomic forms can be put in a grid layout with some labels (see Figure 8.2):

grid′ 5 5 [[*label′* "name :",   *entry′* [] *name*   ]
        , [*label′* "nr. of tickets :", *spinCtrl′* 1 6 [] *nr*]
        ]

Note that the two reference values (*name* :: *Ref m String*) and (*nr* :: *Ref m Int*) are free variables in this expression. Also, this form's subject type is not yet established. To complete the form composition, *name* and *nr* are bound in a lambda expression, onto which a *subject type combinator*, namely *declare2*, is applied:

ticketsForm :: *Monad m* ⇒ *Ref m* (*String*, *Int*) → *FForm win m Layout*
ticketsForm = *declare2* $ λ(*name*, *nr*) →
    grid′ 5 5 [[*label′* "name :",   *entry′* [] *name*   ]
            , [*label′* "nr. of tickets :", *spinCtrl′* 1 6 [] *nr*]
            ]

---
[1] instead of on *Layout* values of widgets – for those familiar with wxHaskell

FIGURE 8.3. *contactForm*₁

This 'declares' *ticketsForm*'s subject type to be (*String, Int*), as witnessed by
its actual type declaration (which can be omitted). Just like the atomic forms,
ticketsForm can now be used as a component of a larger form. Note how this
two-stage process of form construction separates the definition of layout and subject type structures, providing a great deal of freedom to the library user (see
also [EAK05]).

Besides *declare2*, which declares a pair, the library also provides subject type
combinators for tuples of higher arity and for lists.

> *declare2* :: *Monad m* ⇒
> $((Ref\ m\ t_1, Ref\ m\ t_2) \to z)$ → $Ref\ m\ (t_1, t_2) \to z$
> *declare3* :: *Monad m* ⇒
> $((Ref\ m\ t_1, Ref\ m\ t_2, Ref\ m\ t_3) \to z) \to Ref\ m\ (t_1, t_2, t_3) \to z$
> ...
> *declareL* :: *Monad m* ⇒
> $([Ref\ m\ t] \to z)$ → $Ref\ m\ [t] \to z$

The *declareL* combinator only composes forms for the list *elements* and cannot
alter the spine; it produces a form for lists of a fixed length.

To run a form in a wxHaskell program, the library function *runInDialog* is
used. For example, this runs the above defined *ticketsForm* with *John* and *2* in the
atomic forms:

> **do** ...
>   (*newname, newnr*) ← *runInDialog parentWindow ticketsForm* ("John", 2)
>   ...

The function takes as its arguments a pointer to a parent window, the form itself,
and an initial value of the form's subject type. It returns an IO action, which
produces a modal dialog containing the form and *OK/Cancel* buttons. When the
user presses *OK*, the return value is bound to altered value in the form; if *Cancel*
is pressed, the initial value is returned instead. After this, the IO thread continues.

8.3 COMBINATORS FOR DISJOINT FORMS

This section describes, from a library user's point of view, the additions for defining disjoint forms. As an example, we will define a form for contact information,
depicted in Figure 8.3. It has subject type

data *Contact* $=$ *ByPhone Phone* | *ByEmail String* | *NotAtAll*

and expresses a choice between a phone number, an email address and no information at all. Before we can start defining the form itself, we need to define three
custom subject type combinators for this type's data constructors. This is done
using a Template Haskell [SP02] macro named *declare*, which is included in the
library.

$declareByPhone =$ $\$(\underline{declare} \, [|ByPhone|] \, 1)$
$declareByEmail \, =$ $\$(\underline{declare} \, [|ByEmail|] \, 1)$
$declareNotAtAll =$ $\$(\underline{declare} \, [|NotAtAll|] \, 0)$

For each of the constructors, we provide the macro with its name and arity. The
delimiters $\$(\ldots)$ and $[|\ldots|]$ are Template Haskell syntax, which the library user
does not need to worry about.[2]

The three fresh subject type combinators are used to turn forms with subject
types (respectively) *Phone*, *String* and no subject type at all into forms with subject type *Contact*. Their type signatures are:

$declareByPhone :: Monad\ m \Rightarrow$
$\qquad\qquad (Ref\ m\ Phone \, \rightarrow z) \, \rightarrow Ref\ m\ Contact \, \rightarrow z$
$declareByEmail :: Monad\ m \Rightarrow$
$\qquad\qquad (Ref\ m\ String \, \rightarrow z) \, \rightarrow Ref\ m\ Contact \, \rightarrow z$
$declareNotAtAll :: Monad\ m \Rightarrow$
$\qquad\qquad FForm\ win\ m\ l \, \rightarrow Ref\ m\ Contact \, \rightarrow FForm\ win\ m\ l$

In the last type signature, the type *FForm win m l* plays the same role as *z* in the
above signatures. The reason why it is more constrained is that *declareNotAtAll*
appends its argument form with an invisible form for handling the *NotAtAll* value.

Using these subject type combinators, $contactForm_1$ can be defined as follows; we assume (*phoneForm* :: *Ref m Phone* $\rightarrow$ *FForm win m Layout*) is defined somewhere else:

$contactForm_1 = \underline{radioGrid}\ [byPhone, byEmail, byNothing]$
$byPhone \qquad = declareByPhone\ \$\ \lambda phone \rightarrow$
$\qquad\qquad\qquad \underline{row}'\ 5\ [\underline{label}'\ "by\ phone\ :",\ phoneForm\ phone]$
$byEmail \qquad = declareByEmail\ \$\ \lambda email \rightarrow$
$\qquad\qquad\qquad \underline{row}'\ 5\ [\underline{label}'\ "by\ email\ :",\ \underline{entry}'\ [\,]\ email]$
$byNothing \quad\ = declareNotAtAll\ \$$
$\qquad\qquad\qquad \underline{label}'\ "do\ not\ contact\ me"$

The new disjoint form combinator *radioGrid* arranges its list of subforms into
a grid layout, with radio buttons to the left of them. Due to their subject type

---

[2]Template Haskell is a GHC compiler extension for meta-programming, i.e.
programmatically manipulating a program at the syntactic level. The delimiters turn a
meta-language expression into an object-language expression and vice versa. Both object
language and meta-language are Haskell.

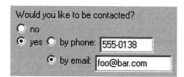

FIGURE 8.4. *contactForm₂*   **FIGURE 8.5.** *contactForm₃*

combinators, the three subforms have the same subject type as the composite form (*Contact*), but each only 'works' for a particular data constructor. For example, the *byEmail* form only handles *ByEmail* values. This means that when *contactForm*₁ is run with an initial *ByEmail* value, the middle radio button is selected, and only the text field next to it receives an initial value. The other text field is left empty (or contains a default value, if the programmer has specified this in *phoneForm*). When the form is closed, every subform contains a final value with its particular *Contact* data constructor, but only one of them is promoted to *contactForm*₁'s final value; this choice is determined by the radio button selected at that time.

What is the advantage of using the disjoint form combinator *radioGrid*, apart from stylistic arguments? Consider the alternative case, in which the form in Figure 8.3 is defined as a *conjunction* of a *radioBox'* (with an *Int* for three possible choices), a *phoneForm* and an *entry'*; its subject type would be (*Int, Phone, String*). At some later time, the interaction design department decides the form should rather look like Figure 8.4 or like Figure 8.5. Note that these forms still express exactly the same choice. However, when the form code is changed accordingly, its subject type would be (*Int, Int, Phone, String*) or (*Bool, Int, Phone, String*), and the code which handles the form data should also be altered.

If we use disjoint forms instead, the disjoint subject type can remain the same. In the code, we only need to add an extra *radioGrid* for the first case:

$$contactForm_2 = \underline{radioGrid}$$
$$[noContact, \lambda yes \rightarrow \underline{row'} \ 5 \ [\underline{label'} \ "yes", \ yesContact \ yes]]$$
$$noContact \quad = declareNotAtAll \ \$ \ \underline{label'} \ "no"$$
$$yesContact \quad = \underline{radioGrid} \ [byPhone, byEmail]$$

For the second case, we use another disjoint form combinator, namely *checkRow*:

$$contactForm_3 = \underline{checkRow}$$
$$(\lambda yes \rightarrow \underline{column'} \ 5 \ [\underline{label'} \ "Please \ contact \ me", \ yesContact \ yes])$$
$$(declareNotAtAll \ \underline{noLayout})$$

The functionality of these forms is still the same: they display a value of their subject type *Contact*, and allow the user to change it into another value of that type.

8.4 IMPLEMENTATION

Although the user of FunctionalForms does not notice a difference, apart from the new combinators and slightly altered *Ref* and *FForm* types, the implementation of the library has undergone substantial changes since its first version in [EAK05]. These allow for generalized forms, which may *fail* to consume an initial value (or produce a final value), and which can be joined with the disjoint form combinators *radioGrid* and *checkRow*. To construct these forms, the *compositional functional references* have also been generalized. Furthermore, the 'heart' of a form, which determines the communication with its environment, has been made explicit in a type *RefLink*. In order to deal with the new *FForm* type in Section 8.4.3, we will first discuss these *Ref* and *RefLink* types.

8.4.1 The *Ref* type

A reference value consists of two functions which are used to 'refer to' a t part of a – usually stateful – monad m:

$$\textbf{data } Ref\ m\ t\ =\ Ref\ \{\ val\ ::\ m\ t \\ ,\ app\ ::\ (t \rightarrow m\ t) \rightarrow m\ () \\ \}$$

The *val* function retrieves the value of this particular part of the monadic state, whereas the *app* function updates it. For example, for a state of type (t_1, t_2), the value referring to the t_1 element would be:

$$reffst\ ::\ MonadState\ (t_1, t_2)\ m\ \Rightarrow\ Ref\ m\ t_1 \\ reffst\ =\ Ref\ \{\ val\ =\ \textbf{do}\ \{\ (x, y)\ \leftarrow\ get;\ return\ x\ \} \\ ,\ app\ =\ \lambda f \rightarrow\ \textbf{do}\ \{\ \tilde{}(x, y)\ \leftarrow\ get;\ x'\ \leftarrow\ f\ x;\ put\ (x', y)\ \} \\ \}$$

Note the lazy pattern match in the *app* function; it is useful when constructing a new state from scratch (i.e. the previous state contains $\perp$).

A reference to the value in a *Just* data constructor (from the well-known *Maybe* type) can be defined in a very similar way:

$$reffromJust\ ::\ MonadState\ (Maybe\ t)\ m\ \Rightarrow\ Ref\ m\ t \\ reffromJust\ =\ Ref \\ \{\ val\ =\ \textbf{do}\ \{\ Just\ x\ \leftarrow\ get;\ return\ x\ \} \\ ,\ app\ =\ \lambda f \rightarrow\ \textbf{do}\ \{\ \tilde{}(Just\ x)\ \leftarrow\ get;\ x'\ \leftarrow\ f\ x;\ put\ (Just\ x')\ \} \\ \}$$

This reference value may seem ill-defined because it can 'dangle': when the monadic state contains *Nothing*, it does not refer to anything. However, this situation can be detected using monadic error-handling, and the control flow can be adapted. We will show how this is done in Section 8.4.2, when we join two *RefLinks*.

The operator • composes two reference values, taking the referred part of the second value's state as the state of the first value. For example, the following value refers to the first element of a pair within a *Just* value:

$$\textit{reffst} \bullet \textit{reffromJust} :: \textit{MonadState}\ (\textit{Maybe}\ (t_1, t_2))\ m \Rightarrow \textit{Ref}\ m\ t_1$$

The composition is performed by applying a monad transformer to the monad of the second reference value. This 'adds state' to this monad, on which the first reference value can act. Meanwhile, properties of the original monad such as IO ability or error handling are preserved.

$$\bullet :: \textit{Monad}\ m \Rightarrow \textit{Ref}\ (\textit{StateT}\ cx\ m)\ t \rightarrow \textit{Ref}\ m\ cx \rightarrow \textit{Ref}\ m\ t$$
$$w \bullet v = \textit{Ref}$$
$$\{\ val\ =\ val\ v \ggg \textit{evalStateT}\ (val\ w)$$
$$,\ app\ =\ \lambda f \rightarrow (app\ v)\ \$\ \textit{execStateT}\ \$\ (app\ w)\ \$\ \textit{lift}\ .\ f$$
$$\}$$

This operator is used to define subject type combinators like:

$$\underline{\textit{declare2}} :: \textit{Monad}\ m \Rightarrow$$
$$((\textit{Ref}\ m\ t_1,\ \textit{Ref}\ m\ t_2) \rightarrow z) \rightarrow \textit{Ref}\ m\ (t_1, t_2) \rightarrow z$$
$$\underline{\textit{declare2}}\ \textit{refsToForm}\ \textit{refP}\ =\ \textit{refsToForm}\ (\textit{reffst} \bullet \textit{refP},\ \textit{refsnd} \bullet \textit{refP})$$

$$\underline{\textit{declareJust}} :: \textit{Monad}\ m \Rightarrow (\textit{Ref}\ m\ a \rightarrow z) \rightarrow \textit{Ref}\ m\ (\textit{Maybe}\ a) \rightarrow z$$
$$\underline{\textit{declareJust}}\ \textit{refToForm}\ \textit{refMaybe}\ =\ \textit{refToForm}\ (\textit{reffromJust} \bullet \textit{refMaybe})$$

These subject type combinators all follow the same pattern. This pattern is captured in the Template Haskell macro *declare*, so definitions like the two above do not have to be handwritten for every data constructor.

8.4.2   The *RefLink* type

The heart of an atomic form consists of a link between two reference values. The first is of type *Ref m t*, and relates the subject type *t* of this form to that of the topmost form (the state type in *m*). This is the reference value that is explicitly provided by the library user, e.g. in the expression $\underline{\textit{entry'}}\ [\ ]\ \textit{ref}_m$. The second reference value is implicit in every atomic form; it is of type *Ref IO t*, and relates this form's subject type to a part of the IO state. It is constructed from wxHaskell's *get* and *set* functions for the control's main attribute (e.g. *text* on an *entry* control).

In the terminology of the well-known model–view(–controller) paradigm [KP88], the reference values refer to a part of the topmost form's *model* and a part of its *view*, respectively. Joining them in a *RefLink* means linking those parts to each other: the *val* output from the first reference is used as *app* input for the second, and vice versa. Thus, two operations are obtained which both enforce consistency between model and view:

- The *update* operation copies the value from the form's model to its view. This is used to show the form's initial value.

- The *propagate* operation copies the value from the form's view to its model. This is used to read the form's final value.

In monadic terms, the *update* operation is a read action in the *m* monad producing a write action in the *IO* monad. Conversely, the *propagate* operation is a read action in the *IO* monad producing a write action in the *m* monad. This results in the following type for *RefLink* (where the *n* monad abstracts from *IO*):

data *RefLink m n* $=$ *RefLink*
  $\{$ *update*   :: $m\,(n\,())$
  , *propagate* :: $n\,(m\,())$
  $\}$

The function *refLink* connects the two references to create such a *RefLink*. For the *update* function, first an input v is retrieved from the *m* reference. Then, a constant function *const* (*return v*) is applied to the corresponding part in the *n* monad using the *n* reference; this action in the *n* monad is returned in the *m* monad. For the *propagate* function, the roles of *m* and *n* are reversed:

refLink :: (*Monad m*, *Monad n*) $\Rightarrow$ *Ref m a* $\to$ *Ref n a* $\to$ *RefLink m n*
refLink ref$_m$ ref$_n$ $=$ *RefLink*
  $\{$ *update* $=$ (*val ref$_m$*) $\gg=$ *return* . (*app ref$_n$*) . *const* . *return*
  , *propagate* $=$ (*val ref$_n$*) $\gg=$ *return* . (*app ref$_m$*) . *const* . *return*
  $\}$

When two forms are joined, their *RefLink*s are combined into a new *RefLink*. Usually, the intention is that the joint *update* performs *both* component *update*s, and likewise for the *propagate*s. We consider this to be the 'default' operator on *RefLink*. In order to meet the *MonadWriter* interface (see Section 8.4.3), we encode it using the *Monoid* class:

instance (*Monad m*, *Monad n*) $\Rightarrow$ *Monoid* (*RefLink m n*)
  where *mempty* $=$ *RefLink*
        $\{$ *update* $=$ *return* $\$$ *return* ()
        , *propagate* $=$ *return* $\$$ *return* ()
        $\}$
    rl$_1$ '*mappend*' *rl$_2$* $=$ *RefLink*
        $\{$ *update* $=$ *liftM2* ($\gg$) (*update rl$_1$*) (*update rl$_2$*)
        , *propagate* $=$ *liftM2* ($\gg$) (*propagate rl$_1$*) (*propagate rl$_2$*)
        $\}$

For disjoint forms, the two *RefLink*s should be joined in an alternative way. In this situation, they share one part of the model part, which is a disjoint union (e.g. the subject type of both forms is *Either a b*). Meanwhile, they refer to different parts of the view (which contains controls for both *a* and *b*). Hence, the two

*RefLink*s connect independent parts of the view state space to 'competing' parts of the model state space. Instead of performing both *update* (*propagate*) operations, only one can (should) be performed.

We obtain this behaviour by using the *mplus* operator of the model monad *m*; therefore, this should be an instance of *MonadPlus*. The joint *update* will then (dynamically) choose between the first component *update* or the second – and likewise for *propagate*. Hence, we define an alternative monoid on the *RefLink* domain. By using a different representation for the *RefLink* type, the *Monoid* class can again be used for this:

newtype *RefLinkPlusM m n* = *RefLinkPlusM* {*pm* :: *RefLink m n*}
instance (*MonadPlus m*, *Monad n*) ⇒ *Monoid* (*RefLinkPlusM m n*) **where**
  mempty = *RefLinkPlusM* $ *RefLink*
    { *update*   = *mzero*
    , *propagate* = *return mzero*
    }
  rl_1 '*mappend*' rl_2 = *RefLinkPlusM* $ *RefLink*
    { *update*   = (*update* $ *pm* rl_1) '*mplus*' (*update* $ *pm* rl_2)
    , *propagate* = *liftM2 mplus* (*propagate* $ *pm* rl_1) (*propagate* $ *pm* rl_2)
    }

The exact semantics of *mplus* depend on the monad *m*. In practice, we use an error-handling state monad *ErrorT e* (*State a*). This means that the first argument of *mplus* is always tried first; if it fails, the second argument is tried. When disjoint forms are used correctly, the alternatives are mutually exclusive, so this order is irrelevant.

8.4.3   The *FForm* type

A form is a value of the following type:

newtype *FForm win m a* = *FForm*
  { *runFForm* :: *Window win* → *IO* (*a*, *RefLink m IO*) }

It contains three pieces of information:

1. An IO action which creates the form's controls. This action depends on a pointer to a parent window of type *Window win*, in which they are created.

2. A *RefLink* used to update the values in the controls from, and propagate them to, the form's model.

3. Additional information of type *a*; usually layout information of type *Layout* (defined by the wxHaskell library).

The *FForm* type can be used as a monad, which *binds* the additional (layout) information, *reads* the window pointer, *executes* the control creation functions, and *writes* a *RefLink*.

$instance\ (Monad\ m)\ \Rightarrow\ Monad\ (FForm\ win\ m)$
$instance\ (Monad\ m)\ \Rightarrow\ MonadReader\ (Window\ win)\ (FForm\ win\ m)$
$instance\ (Monad\ m)\ \Rightarrow\ MonadIO\ (FForm\ win\ m)$
$instance\ (Monad\ m)\ \Rightarrow\ MonadWriter\ (RefLink\ m\ IO)\ (FForm\ win\ m)$

So, $form_1 \ggeq f$ means:

- f is applied to the additional information from $form_1$, producing (let's call it) $form_2$.

- The window pointer passed to $form_1 \ggeq f$ is passed to $form_1$ and $form_2$.

- The IO actions in $form_1$ and $form_2$ are sequenced.

- The *RefLink* in $form_2$ is joined to the *RefLink* in $form_1$ using the 'default' *mappend* operator.

Furthermore, functions like *ask* (extract the window pointer), *liftIO* (insert an IO action at form creation time) and *tell* (insert a *RefLink*) are implemented for the *FForm* monad (being an instance of *MonadReader*, *MonadIO* and *MonadWriter*).

We stated in Section 8.4.2 that in order to combine two forms in a disjoint way, the *RefLinkPlusM* monoid should be used, which dynamically performs *one* of the *update/propagate* operations. Meanwhile, *both* forms should be shown: at form creation time, *both* IO actions should be performed, and *both* layout values are used. Therefore, we have implemented alternative bind and unit operators for forms: $\ggeq\pm$ and $return^0$. They are similar to $\ggeq$ and *return* in every respect, except that they use the *RefLinkPlusM* monoid.

$return^0 :: MonadPlus\ m\ \Rightarrow\ a\ \rightarrow\ FForm\ win\ m\ a$
$(\ggeq\pm)\ :: MonadPlus\ m\ \Rightarrow$
$\qquad\qquad FForm\ win\ m\ a\ \rightarrow\ (a\ \rightarrow\ FForm\ win\ m\ b)\ \rightarrow\ FForm\ win\ m\ b$

These operators are at the core of the disjoint form combinators *radioGrid* and *checkRow*, whose implementation is discussed in the next section.

8.4.4 Disjoint form combinators

A naïve disjoint form combinator would be:

$refToForm_1\ `or`\ refToForm_2\ =\ \lambda ref\ \rightarrow$
$\quad refToForm_1\ ref\ \ggeq\pm\ \lambda lay_1\ \rightarrow$
$\quad refToForm_2\ ref\ \ggeq\pm\ \lambda lay_2\ \rightarrow$
$\quad return^0\ \$\ column\ 5\ [lay_1, lay_2]$

The composite form shows both forms, while the composite *update* function performs only one of the component *update* functions – the first one that succeeds. The same goes for the composite *propagate* operation. However, the form's user has no means whatsoever to discover which *update* has been performed, or to influence which *propagate* to perform![3]

The _radioGrid_ combinator does provide these functions: both are fulfilled by the radio buttons. When a subform's *update* is performed, the system selects the radio button in front of it. Conversely, the form's *propagate* is only performed if the radio button in front of it *is* indeed selected (the user influences this during the form's lifetime).

The nice thing is that we can express this behaviour quite elegantly in terms of *RefLink* operations. We show this by defining the somewhat simpler disjoint form combinator *alt*, which is a specialisation of _radioGrid_: it joins exactly two forms (denoted *refToForm$_1$* and *refToForm$_2$*). Assume that we can create a two-button radio group, returning a reference value *refRadio :: Ref IO Int* to its current selection, which can take values $\{0, 1\}$. Now we can define a *RefLink* value:

$$rl_1 = refLink\ ref0\ refRadio$$
$$\textbf{where}\ ref0 = Ref$$
$$\{\ val = return\ 0$$
$$,\ app = \lambda f \rightarrow \textbf{do}\ \{\ 0 \leftarrow f\ 0;\ return\ ()\ \}$$
$$\}$$

In other words: we link *refRadio* to a reference 'to the unchangeable number 0', whose *val* is always 0, and whose *app* function only succeeds when the result of the function application is 0. This has the effect that the *update* operation in rl_1 always selects the topmost radio button (and succeeds), while its *propagate* operation only succeeds when this radio button is selected.[4]

We then lift rl_1 into a form, and join it with the first subform *form$_1$* using $\gg$, which utilizes the default (conjunctive) *mappend* operator:

$$tell\ rl_1 \gg refToForm_1\ ref$$

This form has the desired properties: with an *update*, the radio button is only selected if the value in *form$_1$* can be updated, and with a *propagate*, the value in *form$_1$* is only propagated if the radio button is selected. We define and use rl_2 in a similar way, producing a second form. We finish the *alt* combinator by joining both forms with $\gg\pm$:

$$refToForm_1\ `alt`\ refToForm_2 = \lambda ref \rightarrow$$
$$\quad liftIO\ \dots \gg= (laybutton_1, laybutton_2, refRadio) \rightarrow$$
$$\quad\quad \textbf{let}$$
$$\quad\quad\quad rl_1 = \dots \quad \text{— see above}$$
$$\quad\quad\quad rl_2 = \dots$$
$$\quad\quad \textbf{in}$$
$$\quad\quad (tell\ rl_1 \gg refToForm_1\ ref) \gg\pm \lambda layform_1 \rightarrow$$
$$\quad\quad (tell\ rl_2 \gg refToForm_2\ ref) \gg\pm \lambda layform_2 \rightarrow$$
$$\quad\quad return^0\ \$\ grid\ 5\ 5\ [[laybutton_1, layform_1], [laybutton_2, layform_2]]$$

---

[3]Both *propagate* operations will succeed when performed. Due to the *mplus* semantics, the first one will always be selected.

[4]Note that this *RefLink* does not use any model state!

What we have omitted in the second line goes into too much implementation detail; it is an IO action which creates the radio buttons, and returns the layout values *laybutton₁* and *laybutton₂*, as well as *refRadio*.

The *radioGrid* combinator is a straightforward generalization of *alt* for lists. The *checkRow* combinator is also very much like *alt*, but does not show its second argument form. However, it *does* use its *RefLink*.[5]

8.5 SAFETY

The flexibility provided by compositional functional references has a downside: by omitting reference values, duplicating them, or using them in the wrong places, forms with strange behaviour can be constructed. We give some examples:

1. *declare2* $\lambda(a,b) \rightarrow$ *entry′* [] *a*

   This form never shows or changes the second element of its subject type.

2. $\lambda a \rightarrow$ *row′* 5 [*entry′* [] *a*, *entry′* [] *a*]

   This form shows its value twice, and only propagates the new value in the control on the right.

3. *declareJust* $ *entry′* []

   This form is only updated if its model contains a *Just x* value (actually, this is the desired behaviour if the form is part of a disjoint form). If it does not, all forms in the same alternative of the surrounding 'disjoint clause' are prevented from being updated (normally, there should be none).

4. *radioGrid* [*entry′* [], *entry′* []]

   This form will always put its value in the upper entry control. However, it will propagate values from whichever entry control has its radio button selected.

To prevent the construction of these forms, the programmer can follow some rules such as:

- Every declared reference should be used exactly once.

- Every data constructor of a form's subject type should be declared exactly once.

- References declared outside a disjoint form must not be used inside it.

Of course, it would be better if these rules would be enforced automatically, e.g. by the type system. Future research should formalize these rules.

---

[5]Its *RefLink* is joined with a *refLink* between the value *False* and the checkbox value.

8.6 RELATED WORK

As far as we know, the idea of explicitly using a radio button grid to combine forms in a disjoint way is new. The fact that some radio buttons make other elements (ir)relevant is recognized, but existing declarative (web) form languages have to go out of their way to specify this. In XForms [XFo], it is accomplished by providing an element's `relevant` property with a Boolean expression that includes an XPath pointer to the radio button choice. In WASH/CGI [Thi02], the programmer builds a *decision tree* (see [Thi03]) to express which data to use when a certain radio button is selected.

A simple disjoint form combinator is already introduced in the thesis [Eve04] from which FunctionalForms originated. However, this combinator always joins exactly two alternative forms. If the subject types of the top form and bottom form are t_1 and t_2, respectively, then the subject type of the composite form is always *Either* t_1 t_2. In other words, logic and layout are not separated like they are presently.

Compositional references were introduced by Kagawa [Kag97] as a means to compose mutable data structures such as arrays. In our previous work [Eve04, EAK05] we used them in a more simple form and with a different goal: to conceptually separate a form's subject type and its layout.

Closely related to compositional references are *lenses* [FGMPS04], which are also pairs of accessor and modificator functions. While our approach uses a lot of 'little' references throughout the program, lenses are combined into a big lens which *is* the program; this program specifies a bidirectional transformation between model and view.

8.7 CONCLUSIONS AND FUTURE WORK

In this paper, we have identified two patterns for composing forms that edit values of a disjoint union type. The first pattern involves a list of radio buttons, and the second involves a check box. To support these patterns in the FunctionalForms library, we have introduced several new combinators.

These patterns illustrate a novel view, in which a form itself can be seen as 'disjoint'. To demonstrate the fertility of this view, we have shown that these disjoint forms exhibit a cleaner separation between logic and user interface. This makes them more flexible.

However, this flexibility comes at a price: the construction of forms with unwanted behaviour is possible. Methods for preventing this have yet to be researched.

As a further enhancement to FunctionalForms, defining forms for values of a custom Haskell type is made easier, using a Template Haskell macro. This brings the library closer to real-life use. The library version discussed in this paper will shortly be available for download.[6]

---

[6]http://www.sandr.dds.nl/FunctionalForms

We hope to further develop the approach of programming with reference values. We believe that it can be used to construct a far wider range of interfaces in a declarative way.

REFERENCES

[Eve04]   Sander Evers.   Form follows function: Editor GUIs in a functional style.   Master's thesis, University of Twente, 2004.   Available at `http://doc.utwente.nl/fid/2101`. Accessed 27 April 2005.

[EAK05]   Sander Evers, Peter Achten, and Jan Kuper.   A functional programming technique for forms in graphical user interfaces. In *Proc. of the 16th International Workshop on Implementation and Application of Functional Languages (IFL 2004)*, vol 3474 of *LNCS*, pages 35–51. Springer-Verlag, Berlin, 2005.

[FGMPS04] J. Nathan Foster, Michael B. Greenwald, Jonathan T. Moore, Benjamin C. Pierce, and Alan Schmitt. Combinators for bi-directional tree transformations: A linguistic approach to the view update problem. Technical Report MS-CIS-04-15, University of Pennsylvania, August 2004. An earlier version appeared in the *Workshop on Programming Language Technologies for XML (PLAN-X)*, 2004, under the title "A Language for Bi-Directional Tree Transformations".

[Pey03]   Simon Peyton Jones. Haskell 98 language and libraries: the revised report. *Journal of Functional Programming*, 13(1):0–255, January 2003.

[Kag97]   Koji Kagawa. Compositional references for stateful functional programming. In *Proc. of the second ACM SIGPLAN International Conference on Functional Programming (ICFP'97)*, vol 32(8) of *SIGPLAN Notices*, pages 217–226. ACM Press, 1997.

[KP88]   Glenn E. Krasner and Stephen T. Pope. A cookbook for using the model-view controller user interface paradigm in smalltalk-80. *J. Object Oriented Program.*, 1(3):26–49, 1988.

[Lei04]   Daan Leijen. wxHaskell – a portable and concise GUI library for Haskell. In *ACM SIGPLAN Haskell Workshop (HW'04)*. ACM Press, September 2004.

[SP02]   Tim Sheard and Simon Peyton Jones.   Template metaprogramming for Haskell.   In Manuel M. T. Chakravarty, editor, *ACM SIGPLAN Haskell Workshop 02*, pages 1–16. ACM Press, October 2002.

[Thi02]   Peter Thiemann. WASH/CGI: Server-side web scripting with sessions and typed, compositional forms. In *Proc. of the 4th International Symposium on Practical Aspects of Declarative Languages*, vol 2257 of *LNCS*, pages 192–208. Springer-Verlag, Berlin, 2002.

[Thi03]   Peter   Thiemann.   An   embedded   domain-specific   language   for   type-safe   server-side   web-scripting.   Technical report,   Universität   Freiburg,   May   2003.   Available   at `http://www.informatik.uni-freiburg.de/~thiemann/papers/`. Accessed 27 April 2005.

[wxW]   wxWidgets home page: `http://www.wxwidgets.org`. Accessed 27 April 2005.

[XFo]   XForms home page: `http://www.w3.org/MarkUp/Forms/`. Accessed 27 April 2005.

Chapter 9

A Graphic Functional-Dataflow Language

Silvia Clerici[1], Cristina Zoltan[1]

Abstract: NiMo (Nets in Motion) is a visual environment aimed to support totally graphic programming in Data Flow style, with a strong functional inspiration. It enables the user to describe solutions of growing complexity using a small set of graphic primitives. The NiMo language allows multiple output channels and adds graphic representation to deal with functional concepts like higher order, partial application, laziness, polymorphism and type inference. The environment is based on a graph transformation system, by means of which execution can be done step-by-step. NiMo intends to be a workbench for editing, debugging, executing and experimenting. Nets are built and run using a uniform conceptual framework. The net to be initially executed is exactly the one drawn by the user. It evolves showing all transformations of data and processes. The most distinguishing characteristic of NiMo is allowing the user to execute incomplete programs and to change the execution state (data, processes and/or control) in an interactive way.

9.1 INTRODUCTION

Functional languages such as Miranda [Tur85] or Haskell [HJW$^+$92, Has04] have powerful primitives for building algorithms in a simple way. Higher order functions are program schemes that allow building software pieces from higher levels of abstraction. Solutions are obtained by the composition of built-in blocks of well-known semantics. Reusability is promoted by defining polymorphic higher

---

[1]Dept. Llenguatges i Sistemes Informàtics Universitat Politècnica de Catalunya Barcelona, Spain; E-mail: {silvia,zoltan}@lsi.upc.edu

order functions that extend the predefined schemes with more specialized ones.

Data flow is a simple and powerful computational model [Den74] that has inspired several visual programming languages. In lazy functional programming, data flow representations visualize the program as a net of communicating processes where functions are processes and channels are (usually infinite) lists. During the last years the interest for visual modelling and programming has progressively grown, giving rise to a wide variety of visual languages and environments [JHM04]. In particular there are a certain number of them close to functional programming or data flow paradigm: Prograph [CGP89], Visual Haskell [Ree94], VFPE [Kel02], Vital [Han02]. They were developed with different objectives and therefore the term 'Visual' has different meanings: graphical edition, visual representations of textual programs, data structures animation, graphical display of the internal representation, visualization of how some part of it evolves during execution, etc. Some of these languages share certain characteristics with NiMo but their specific objectives and the way they are implemented are fairly different.

The main goal in NiMo is to provide totally graphic edition, debugging, execution and experimentation. The source code is a graph, which is directly executable. It is not a graphic representation of the code of a given textual language as it is the case in several visual languages, for instance in Visual Haskell. Although close enough to lazy functional languages NiMo follows a functional-data-flow mix model, and there is no need for the user to write textual code at all. On the other hand, although the graph could be easily translated into a lazy functional language as Miranda or Haskell, this is not the case either. The interpreter acts directly upon the source code, without any kind of translation, by means of a graph transformation system. The execution model in NiMo could be regarded as the visualization process of a graph operational semantics for an equivalent textual program, where the state model is a graph; during execution all the intermediate states are shown, not only the final one.

The NiMo environment, which is described in Section 9.3, is based on a graph transformation system [Roz97]. This means that NiMo implementation is also graphical. It consists of two kernel graph grammars; one of them acts as an interactive syntax directed editor while the other one is the interpreter, which acts directly on the source code. Execution can be done in free mode or step-by-step also allowing incomplete programs to be executed and completed as needed.

There are several tracers for functional programs that also share some functionalities with our work. In particular for the Haskell language we can mention HsDebug [EJ03] for GHC [Com04], HOOD which is a small post-mortem debugger, being enhanced by GHOOD [GHO04]. GHOOD has a very nice interface for visualization of selected elements of the program. All of them require signaling the functions that are to be observed. The main difference with them is that NiMo acts as an online tracer. All the net activity is shown by default; therefore the marking should be for the processes of which we do not want to see the internals. Step-by-step execution allows online debugging and also several kinds of experiments on the running net, like relaxing laziness for some processes, bounding the execution to a particular subnet, analyzing channel population, testing the need of forcing synchronization, etc.

A running prototype has been implemented using AGG [ERT99], [TB04] as the graph transformation system. It is described in Section 9.4 together with its possible extensions.

In the next section the main characteristics of the language are outlined and illustrated by means of simple examples of its use.

9.2   OUTLINE OF THE NIMO LANGUAGE

The language has been designed to support totally graphic programming in Data Flow style, with a strong functional inspiration. It is based on the classical process network representations for lazy functional programs. A small set of graphic primitives allows representing and handling functional concepts like higher order, partial application, laziness, polymorphism, and type inference. The program is a graph drawn by the user, which evolves during execution showing every transformation of data and processes. The most peculiar characteristic of NiMo is that the source code is both the object code and the initial state at the same time. This feature, added to the possibility of executing (may be incomplete) programs step-by-step, enables the user to change the state (data, processes and/or control) at any point. This section outlines the main features of the language and the functional-data-flow mix model it supports, starting with the usual process network representations in which NiMo was inspired.

9.2.1   Data flow representation for lazy functional programs

In the basic data flow model processes are visualized as boxes (nodes), and arrows represent channels where data streams flow from one process to other. The control is given by the flow of data; there are no additional control structures. Data-flow representations have shown to be a useful conceptual mechanism to visualize the behaviour of a certain kind of lazy functional programs. The data flow metaphor

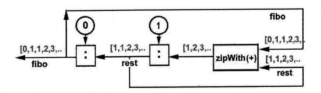

FIGURE 9.1.   Fibonacci process network

associates functions to single output processes and channels to (usually infinite) lists. Net architecture shows in a bi-dimensional way the chains of function compositions and exhibits the implicit parallelism. Back arrows give an insight of the 'recurrence laws', i.e. how new results are obtained from already calculated ones.

The paradigmatic example of such correspondence is Fibonacci. Its process network representation, present in many textbooks on lazy functional programming, and the graphic execution model that the net animation suggests, were the start point for the NiMo language design. Figure 9.1 shows the net corresponding to the Haskell code

```
fibo = 0 :  rest where rest = 1 :  zipWith (+) fibo rest
```

9.2.2 The graphic elements

The graphic syntax in NiMo is very close to the one above. Figure 9.2 shows the Fibonacci net in NiMo.

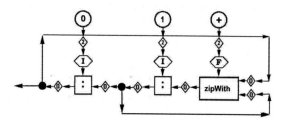

FIGURE 9.2.   Fibonacci process network in NiMo

Except for a few new graphic symbols (hexagons, diamonds, and big-arrows shown in Figure 9.3), the rest of the elements and their correspondence to the textual code are the usual ones:

- Rectangles for functions viewed as processes.

- Circles (or ellipses when necessary) for constant values.

- Arrows for function parameters and result, avoiding the use of the identifiers needed in textual code (*fibo* and *rest* in this example).

- Horizontal arrows to represent channels and black dots for channel duplicators (double occurrence of an identifier in the textual code definition).

- Vertical arrows for those function parameters that are not channels in the data flow sense of flowing data streams.

The diamond symbol is a connector that ties arrows together and carries information about activation or evaluation state. A diamond with 0 precedes a non-activated process or a non-evaluated value. Values in a channel are always preceded by a diamond with code 1. Hexagons carry type information. Data are type-value-entities (*tve*), where values (evaluated or not) are tied to its type (hexagon) through a diamond. Code 2 in the diamond indicates that the value is an atomic constant. Fully evaluated values (values in normal form) are tve's having only hexagons, circles and diamonds. Non-fully evaluated values are tve's containing at least one rectangle (a non-evaluated function), see Figure 9.6. Formal parameters are represented by incomplete tve's; i.e. having big arrows (as shown in Figure 9.3). In fact, big arrows represent incompleteness in a more general sense; they are open connections that can be bound later. Since execution can be done step-by-step, incomplete programs can be executed and completed by need.

NiMo allows full higher order parameterization and partial application. Process parameters can also be parameterized; i.e. not only function names as +, but also partially applied functions (a box with big-arrows in some of its inputs) can be a valid parameter for another process, see the net *quickSrec* in Figure 9.7. Furthermore, processes in NiMo can have multiple outputs, but only single output processes can be a valid parameter. In other words, functions can be viewed as processes when applied, but multiple output processes cannot be viewed as functions.

9.2.3 The type system

Atomic types are integers (I), reals (R), booleans (B), strings (S). Circles of different colours represent constant values of each type.

Structured types are lists (L), channels (C), tuples (T), and functions (F) all being polymorphic. Channels and lists are homogeneous and unbounded. They correspond to the data flow and functional view of lists and therefore they are mutually convertible.

In the current version user defined types are not supported. On the other hand, there is only one function type name F standing for the type $a \rightarrow b$, only one list type name L for lists of any kind of elements, and the only polymorphic type identifier is ?. The type List of integer, for instance, corresponds to a *list-tve* (a tve with L in its hexagon) with *integer-tve's* as elements of its (structured) value. Therefore only lists having a first concrete typed element show they are concrete; an empty list or a non-evaluated one (not in w.h.n.f.) is, in principle, polymorphic. The same happens with channels. As a consequence, static type inference is partial, which means that polymorphic processes could be non-correctly instantiated and therefore non type-safe nets could be executed. Type inference and checking at runtime is therefore needed (see Section 9.3.1 for further discussion). In the NiMo next version (under preparation) full static inference will be possible.

9.2.4 Basic processes and nets

As said before, NiMo language was designed to support the data flow process network programming style. The system provides a repertory of powerful *basic processes* including equivalent versions for most functions in Haskell prelude. It also includes additional higher order processes that facilitate the static process network style, like a generalized zipWith-merge, a flip-flop-merge, or a fixpoint process. But with some of the Haskell functions (like splitAt, span, or break) the equivalence is not exact because processes in NiMo can have more than one output channel, which can be independently activated (like the process splitCond in

Figure 9.7). Process network solutions obtained using these primitives as basic processes avoid the use of tuples and projections or 'symmetric duplication' of processes, which are needed to simulate two output branches in Haskell. In fact, tuples are only used in NiMo when dealing with truly Cartesian Product elements, and could be simulated by the multiple outputs of a process. On the other hand, additional graphic syntax for conditional, guards or case expressions is not either really necessary: an if-then-else higher order process suffices for handling all the conditional situations. The idea is that casuistic and pattern decomposition are encapsulated within the basic processes behaviour. Basic processes are powerful enough to handle stream processing in the data flow sense; only the simplest user functions (i.e. not involving control flow) should need conditionals. This restriction enforces a static network solution style, without explicit recursivity in processes; recurrence is done on channels (feed back arrows). In this kind of solutions the total number of processes is statically bounded. During execution the net structure is similar to the original one, regarding the processes and their interconnections, only new values are dynamically generated in channels (as in the case of the net *prefixes*, explained in the next sections). However, as it is discussed in Section 9.2.6, dynamic nets can also be represented in NiMo. In this case, a graphic syntax for channel patterns would be helpful to define recursive nets.

Anyhow, the user builds solutions combining processes that can be basic or net themselves. Every new net can be named to be used by another one, allowing incremental net complexity up to any arbitrary degree, and nets can also be parameterized. Figure 9.3 shows the net that generalizes the Fibonacci algorithm to obtain successions where the first and second elements, and the function to apply to the two previous values, are formal parameters. Some useful parameterized nets are provided in a library that can be extended with user-defined nets.

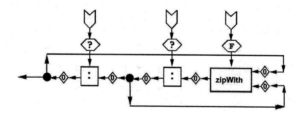

FIGURE 9.3.   Generalized Fibonacci process network

9.2.5   The execution model

In functional languages the execution model strongly depends on the overall evaluation policy. In general, it can be lazy or eager (although efficiency reasons can relax the 'purity' of the evaluation order). In lazy languages there are primitives to annotate a sub expression to be eagerly evaluated; it is the only way the user can explicitly modify the control. On the contrary, in NiMo each subnet is explicitly preceded by its evaluation state, and the user can set an initial activation or change the current activation state of any process during execution. Nevertheless, the default policy is lazy; basic processes have a lazy behaviour, activation propagates by need and persists until an 'sufficiently evaluated' result is obtained. Therefore, provided that the net initial marking only activates the output channels, and that all its sub-nets have a lazy behaviour, the net itself will have a lazy behaviour. However other possible markings could also respect laziness, as it is discussed in Section 9.2.6 for the net in Figure 9.9.

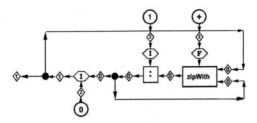

FIGURE 9.4.   Fibonacci first step

In the basic data flow model, control is data driven, i.e. processes act by data availability. In the mix model, laziness means that processes only produce results under demand, i.e. the control flow follows a demand-driven policy (the only exception to this rule appears when simplification keeps semantics). Therefore, executing the Fibonacci net requires creating a demand on its output channel, i.e. setting 1 in its preceding diamond. The first process ':' acts putting its parameter on its output channel and then disappears; the resulting net is shown in 9.4.

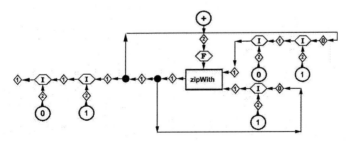

FIGURE 9.5.   Fibonacci third value required

This first value 0 is then shown as the first result and it is also duplicated, being so available in the first input channel of zipWith. Value entities in a channel are always preceded by a diamond with code 1. Figures 9.5 and 9.6 show the net before and after the third value is calculated. In the general case, an activated process can demand non-available values to its provider processes, which are activated 'in parallel' (all that needed, not only the 'leftmost one', as in sequential lazy languages) and, in turn, activate their own providers. Then, process activation can propagate and therefore several processes could work simultaneously in different regions of the net. In the current implementation, this means that whenever two processes are activated, the application order is non deterministic, as it is further discussed in Section 9.3.2. In NiMo most basic processes only act when their preceding diamonds have code 1, (as it was the case for zipWith). However, due to efficiency reasons, some processes could act without being activated (e.g. + whenever its two operands are available, or *map* with an empty input channel). Once activated, a basic process has a lazy behaviour; it only propagates activation in the input channels it needs to produce its result, i.e. to put a next value on every activated output channel; then it becomes deactivated (all its preceding diamond have a 0-value). In other words, processes act until a w.h.n.f. is obtained in each activated output channel.

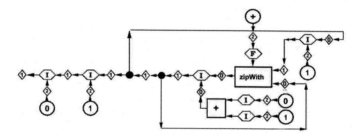

FIGURE 9.6.   Fibonacci third value produced

In order to allow a process to be continuously activated, NiMo provides a basic process *force*, which generates a continuous demand on its input channel and also a process *force-eval* that, in addition, completely evaluates its input. Besides, as execution can be done step-by-step, the user can activate/deactivate any process, by simply changing the code of its preceding diamond. This facility opens a wide range of experimental possibilities not present in the off line style debuggers because some regions of the net can be tested in an isolated manner at any point of the execution. Moreover, relaxing laziness online allows to explore possible optimizations and to analyze synchronization issues. It also enables parallel execution of subnets that, following the default lazy policy, should remain inactive.

9.2.6   Drawing dynamic nets

As we have pointed out in Section 9.2.4, static net programming style promotes the intensive use of built-in recursive patterns, and therefore channel pattern is not really needed. On the contrary, to draw dynamic nets it is convenient to have a more specialized syntax than the generic if-then-else basic process. Figure 9.7 shows the pair of (mutually recursive) nets for the quicksort algorithm. The net *quickSort* shows the graphic syntax for channel patterns, where upper or lower processes enclosed between triangles will be applied depending respectively whether the channel is empty or not. In execution, the sub graph between diamonds is replaced by one of the two processes. In this example *quickSrec* deals with the non empty case; afterwards it is replaced by its net which contains two new processes *quickSort*. This indirect recursion is necessary whenever the end of the recursion is given by a channel pattern; otherwise (for instance in the dynamical version of the Eratosthenes sieve), a single recursive net is enough. The basic process *splitCond* in the net *quickSrec* can be simulated in Haskell by a pair of symmetric filters giving both partitions of the input channel according to the condition and its negation. The big arrow in the $>=$ process corresponds to the parameter of the (a $>=$) section in the Haskell code, being a, the first value in the input channel. The equivalent Haskell code for both nets is the following:

```
quickSort [ ] = [ ]
quickSort(a:x) = quickSrec(a:x)
quickSrec(a:x) = quickSort(filter(a>=)x)++
                (a:quickSort(filter(a<)x))
```

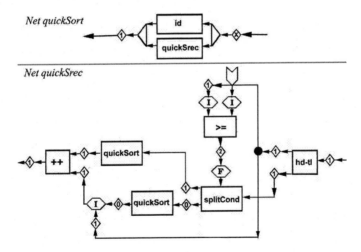

FIGURE 9.7.   Dynamic solution for the quicksort algorithm

Let us note that the initial activation marking (diamonds preceding processes) of the net *quickSrec* preserves laziness. The sequence of diamonds with code 1 is exactly the one that would result by propagating the activation from the leftmost diamond (the one preceding the process ++). According to this, the lower *quick-Sort* process in the net will not be activated until the upper one completes its task (because ++ first consumes completely its first input channel). A possible experiment is to activate also the second *quickSort*, allowing that both processes can act at the same time. This action should also affect the distribution of channel population. In general, trying different markings on the net dynamically allows, for instance, to extend the implicit parallelism in order to speed-up the system behaviour in a further parallel implementation. Also, both the full vision of the state and the step-by-step execution enable the user to experiment even by changing values online.

Execution of both *quicksort* algorithm versions and other examples can be found in [NiM05].

9.3   THE NIMO ENVIRONMENT

NiMo has been developed with the goal of being a workbench for graphically editing, debugging and executing process network solutions. Nets are built and executed using a uniform conceptual framework. As in Functional Languages, where everything is an expression (data, processes, and also the program being executed), in NiMo everything is a graph. Graph grammars and graph transformation systems are powerful tools to deal with graphs. The NiMo environment is based on a graph transformation system that allows rule application to be done step-by-step or in free mode. It has two kernel attributed graph grammars: *Construction Grammar (CGG)*, and *Execution Grammar (EGG)*. EGG is the interpreter, and also gives the complete semantic definition of the language, while CGG acts as an interactive syntax directed editor that checks a first level of type-consistency.

9.3.1   Editing nets

In functional languages, the program is usually edited in a regular text editor and the whole text is compiled. The type inference system deals with the complete internal representation. On the contrary, in NiMo partial type checking and inference are made step-by-step, and locally, during the net edition. On the other hand, Graph Grammar based syntax checkers use techniques for 'scanning' a graph to verify the abstract syntax graph is not violated. In other cases the technique is checking if the 'graph can be parsed'. The first approach is incomplete and the second is not step-by-step. In NiMo nets are constructed using the grammar CGG, its rules can assure a valid graph at each construction step.

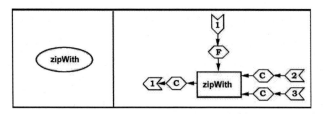

FIGURE 9.8.   Interface rule for zipWith

Every basic process or net in the system has an *interface rule* giving its type declaration (input and output channels and parameters types). For example, the interface rule for the zipWith process is shown in Figure 9.8. During the net edition, adding a new process (basic or net) requires to create a circle, and to fill it in with the process name. The interface rule creates a template with the process graphic signature in the working graph. The new output big-arrows can be connected with the existing input ones, provided that their types are compatible. A set of rules handles partial type checking and inference. Partial means that in the presence of two polymorphic types (big-arrows having a non concrete type identifier in the hexagon) a non-safe connection could be allowed. For instance a first zipWith that (according to its functional parameter once it is connected) requires a first input channel of integer values, could be connected with a second zipWith that, according to its functional parameter, returns a boolean channel. This type inconsistence will be detected in execution when the first functional parameter is applied.

Once a new net is built, it can be directly executed or else be given a name to be further used. This action generates two new rules, an *interface rule* and an *expansion rule* like the one in Figure 9.9. The interface rule allows to construct other nets that have it as a process. It is also used in execution to allow higher order parameterization as described in Section 9.3.2. The expansion rule will be added to EGG to be used while executing a net having a box with the same name. When this process is activated, its whole net (the one on the right of the expansion rule) replaces the box that already has the necessary connections. Figure 9.9 shows the expansion rule for the net *prefixes*, which generates the list of all the initial sub-lists of a given list. This is one of the useful nets provided in the library.

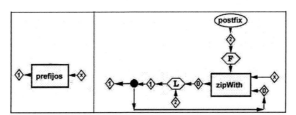

FIGURE 9.9. **Expansion rule for the net prefixes**

9.3.2   Executing nets

As stated before, one of the most distinguishing characteristics of NiMo is that source code is not transformed to start execution; it is the object code itself. At the beginning of the execution the net is exactly the one drawn by the user, and EGG acts directly on it. In execution the net shrinks and expands following the evaluation needs. Diamond nodes keep track of process activation state or evaluation degree for values. Therefore, rules are applicable only on active regions of the net. If more than one process is active, rule application, being non-deterministic, gives a good simulation (the visual effect) of concurrency.

Along with this, the graph transformation system not only provides mechanisms for interrupting execution, running the net in step-by-step mode, and undoing transformation steps but also allows modifying the net at any stage and resuming execution thereafter.

According to the demand-driven policy, the initial activation of the net is done by activating its output channels (although a different initial marking could be set). From then on, activation is propagated by need, in a waterfall mode. If the first process in a channel is not a basic one, it is expanded, and so on until a basic process can act. Once activated it is responsible for activating its provider processes. Basic process rules give the operative basis for the graphic transformation and moving of data through channels. The set of rules defining the behaviour of a given basic process is analogous to the equations defining a function in Haskell. Different configurations in its adjacent nodes give the patterns.

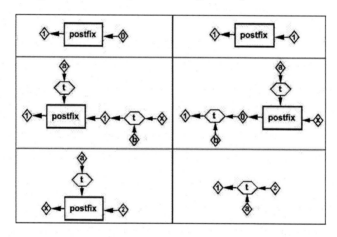

FIGURE 9.10.   Rules for the postfix basic process

Figure 9.10 shows the three rules defining the behaviour of the basic process *postfix* (which adds an element at the end of a list). The first rule activates its provider process, since a 0-value in the input channel diamond indicates that no value was available. The second and third rules correspond, respectively, to the non empty and empty input channel patterns. A diamond with code 2 indicates the end of a channel (or of a list value). In this case, being activated or not (a variable in the preceding diamond) the process generates the last value by putting its parameter in the output channel, and then disappears.

As said before, nets always have two rules (interface and expansion). The net behaviour depends on the internal structure of interconnections among its processes, given by the expansion rule. The interface rule allows that a process or a net (provided it has a single output channel) can act as a process parameter inside other nets. In this context, supporting full higher order implies the dynamic transformation of the net in such a way that a functional parameter (a function name as + in Figure 9.5) can act, i.e. be converted in an executable subnet (as the resulting third value in Figure 9.6). On the other hand partially applied functions (processes having big arrows in some of their entries) can also be a valid parameter or result, and therefore partial parameter passing is also allowed. In EGG a set of only twelve rules handles higher order and partial instantiation in all possible cases. In the presence of processes acting as parameters the application of these rules causes 'internal states' to show up. These intermediate states of the net can be optionally hidden from the user.

Moreover, also functional values in NiMo are first class in the 'showing' sense, allowing incremental development and modular testing of subnets the final results of which contain functional values. For instance, once the net corresponding to the expression `map(zipWith(const id))[[1],[2],[3,4]]` is completely evaluated (no 0-value diamonds remains), it results into a channel of partially instantiated functions representing the expression `[zipwith(const id) [1],zipwith(const id)[2],zipwith(const id)[3,4]]`. On the contrary, in textual languages the expression is considered erroneous, as in Haskell, or else in Miranda the result shown is: `[<function>,<function>,<function>]`.

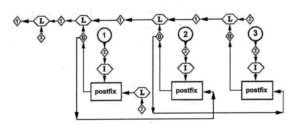

FIGURE 9.11.   Prefixes of the list [1,2,3]

Regarding data, normal order evaluation leads to duplicate sub-expressions. In lazy functional languages identical substructures are evaluated only once using graphs instead of trees as syntax internal representation; several nodes share the same son. Data management policy in NiMo uses the same strategy and is implemented by sharing structured values. That means, that evaluated subnets can not be immediately discarded because they could be shared by another subnet. A set of garbage collector rules in EGG takes care of erasing 'right to left' disconnected (as provider) nodes. This set of rules act 'in parallel' with the rest of the grammar rules. Figure 9.11 displays an intermediate state of the net *prefixes* applied to a finite input channel [1,2,3], exhibiting sub graph sharing.

In EGG, all the previously mentioned tasks are organized into sets of specific purpose rules. Besides, another advantage of having a uniform framework is that program transformation and optimization can be addressed using the same mechanism. A set of rules can do optimization using known patterns. This type of transformations could take place before the execution starts, or even when the pattern shows up due to the net evolution.

9.4 CURRENT STATE AND FUTURE WORK

A running prototype has been implemented using AGG [ERT99], [TB04] as the graph transformation system. Currently, over 20 basic processes including equivalent versions for most useful functions in Haskell prelude are implemented. Real and tuple types are not yet included. A special effort was done in order to reduce the number of rules, keeping always in mind that the system time complexity strongly depends on the grammar size and on the sub-graph matching algorithm being used. The presence of diamonds, gives bipartite sub-graphs, and then heavily reduces the number of rules (patterns in left hand sides). Adding them all up, the sets of rules in EGG are around a hundred. On the other hand, the kernel grammar does not have critical pairs, and only injective match mappings are used, reducing the execution (graph transformation) complexity. Confluence (and therefore rule application order independence) assures a well-defined semantics.

The system has been tested on classical examples as hamming numbers, prime numbers in both static and dynamic versions, prefixes, quicksort in different dynamic and static versions, obtained by derivation from the classical one (Figure 9.7), other sorting algorithms, and of course, Fibonacci.

In order to test full higher order and partial application a set of examples were evaluated, for instance the NiMo nets equivalent to the following Haskell codes

```
zipWith id(map(zipWith(const id)) [[1],[2],[3,4]]) l
where l = [[5], [6,7,8], [9], []]
zipWith id(zipWith const(zipWith id(repeat(+))nat)nat)nat
where nat = [1..]
```

The work done shows the feasibility of the approach and the experimental possibilities it opens. However, although the main design and implementation challenges have been overcome, for the time being, the current state of the system is far from being a final product. One of the main drawbacks of the current version is, precisely, the graphical interface. To be a really useful tool this aspect should be heavily improved. As the net grows, it is necessary to have control on scaling, zooming, scrolling and other facilities allowing 'pretty printing' of the net, not present in the graphic interface of the current transformation system. Nevertheless, the graph transformation engine can be used isolated and be combined with another interface. In fact, graph transformation systems are powerful tools to deal with complex graph configurations but, as far as the authors know, they are not intended to be used as graphical interfaces in a relatively large size application. They are mainly used for modelling. In [NiM05] executions of some of the examples tested in the prototype are shown as they would look like with an improved graphic interface.

Regarding the extension of the language itself, as we said before, a more powerful type inference system is under development. And, in general, other Haskell features not having equivalence in NiMo, should also be considered. In particular, user defined types and therefore data abstractions mechanisms, which are a key issue for scalability [BBB+95]. On this regard, NiMo already has a procedural abstraction mechanism to represent a complex net by a single node, therefore allowing to face more complex problems. But, as in every visual language, as the net grows the limited screen size is a problem that the usual mechanisms (scrolling, zooming, etc.) are not powerful enough to solve. Currently, once expanded a net process remains so whether active or not. A possible approach for a better use of the screen real estate would be to provide operations to reverse the expansion, compress basic type-values, and display a graphic shorthand for numeric lists.

Finally as it can be seen in all the previous examples, translation from NiMo to Haskell is almost direct. NiMo is specially suited for debugging and experimentation, not for being the final execution system. The last step of the workbench should be to produce an equivalent but efficiently executable textual version, ideally in a parallel language.

9.5   CONCLUDING REMARKS

This paper has presented a novel graphical language inspired in the data flow representations for lazy functional programs, and the environment designed to give support to this programming style. The main characteristics of the language have been illustrated with several examples, showing how the program evolves in execution, and the particular kind of interactions the system allows. We have also described the fundamental ideas in the implementation of the environment by means of a graph transformation system, the current state of the implementation, its drawbacks and possible improvements.

The most relevant characteristics of NiMo are:

- It is totally graphic. Programs are graphs drawn by the user, which are directly executable without any kind of translation and evolve showing all transformations of data and processes, allowing online tracing. On the other hand, the environment has been fully implemented using graph grammars, and therefore the implementation of the environment itself is also graphic.

- The language is very simple and expressive, close to the usual data flow representations for lazy functional programs. Nets of growing complexity are built with a small set of graphic primitives. Only seven symbols are enough to represent and handle higher order, partial instantiation, polymorphism, type inference, and keep track of the evaluation state.

- The system provides a repertory of basic processes including equivalent versions of most useful functions in the Haskell prelude, but unlike functional programming, processes can have more than one output channel. This facility avoids the use of tuples and projections or symmetric duplication of processes making clearer the data flow solution.

- And the most innovative one is that the user has direct control on the computation state and can change data, processes and/or control at any point of the execution. This is feasible because of the combination of several peculiarities:

the source code is exactly the computation initial state, the activation or evaluation state is explicit, the execution can be done step-by-step, and between steps the user can modify the net. Therefore, not only online debugging is natural but even, laziness can be locally relaxed in an interactive way.

REFERENCES

[BBB+95]   M. Burnett, M.J. Baker, C. Bohus, P. Carlson, S. Yang, and P. Van Zee. Scaling up visual programming languages. *Computer*, 28:45–54, 1995.

[CGP89]   P. T. Cox, F. R. Giles, and T. Pietrzykowski. Prograph: A step towards liberating programming from textual conditioning. In *IEEE Workshop on Visual Languages*, pages 150–156, 1989.

[Com04]   Glasgow Haskell Compiler. http://www.haskell.org/ghc. 2004.

[Den74]   J. Denis. First version of a data flow procedure language. In *LNCS 19*, Springer-Verlag, Berlin, pages 362–376, 1974.

[EJ03]   Robert Ennals and Simon Peyton Jones. Hsdebug: debugging lazy programs by not being lazy. In *Proceedings of the ACM SIGPLAN workshop on Haskell*, pages 84–87. ACM Press, 2003.

[ERT99]   C. Ermel, M. Rudolf, and G. Taentzer. The agg approach: language and environment. In H. Ehrig, G. Engels, H.-J. Kreowski, and G. Rozenberg, editors, *Handbook of graph grammars and computing by graph transformation: vol. 2*, pages 551–603. World Scientific Publishing Co., Inc., 1999.

[GHO04]   Page GHOOD. http://www.cs.kent.ac.uk/people/staff/cr3/toolbox/haskell/ghood/. Accessed 27 April 2005.

[Han02]   Keith Hanna. Vital interactive visual functional programming. In *Proceedings of the seventh ACM SIGPLAN international conference on Functional programming*, pages 145–156, 2002.

[Has04]   Home Page Haskell. http://www.haskell.org/. Accessed 27 April 2005.

[HJW+92]   P. Hudak, S. Peyton Jones, P. Wadler, et al. Report on the functional programming language haskell: Version 1.2. *ACM SIGPLAN Notices*, 27(5), 1992.

[JHM04]   Wesley M. Johnston, J. R. Paul Hanna, and Richard J. Millar. Advances in dataflow programming languages. *ACM Comput. Surv.*, 36(1):1–34, 2004.

[Kel02]   Joel Kelso. A Visual Programming Environment for Functional Languages. Phd. Thesis Murdoch University, 2002.

[NiM05]   NiMo. The NiMo Home Page. http://www.lsi.upc.edu/~NiMo/Project/, 2005. Accessed 27 April 2005.

[Ree94]   H. Reekie. Visual Haskell: A First Attempt. Technical Report 94.5, University of Technology Sydney, March 1994.

[Roz97]   Grzegorz Rozenberg, editor. *Handbook of Graph Grammars and Computing by Graph Transformations, Volume 1*. World Scientific, 1997.

[TB04]   TU-B. AGG Home Page. http://tfs.cs.tu-berlin.de/agg/. Acc. 27 April 2005.

[Tur85]   D. Turner. Miranda: A non strict functional language with polymorphic types. In *Functional Programming Languages and Computer Architecture, LNCS 201*, Springer-Verlag, Berlin, 1985.